DURHAM CITY

North-east view of the City of Durham.

DURHAM CITY

Keith Proud

Phillimore

1992

Published by
PHILLIMORE & CO. LTD.
Shopwyke Hall, Chichester, Sussex

ISBN 0 85033 824 7

Printed and bound in Great Britain by
BIDDLES LTD.,
Guildford, Surrey

For my wife Barbara, and her infinite patience; for my children, Robin and Rachael; and for my parents, Marjorie and John, who did so much to foster in me a lasting love of this beautiful county.

Contents

List of Illustrations

Frontispiece: North-east view of the city

Acknowledgements

I should like to express my sincere thanks to the following people and organisations for the invaluable help given in the preparation of this book. It was John Donne who first ventured the thesis that 'No man is an island'; rarely has truth been more accurately penned.

My great friend, Neville Turner, took the photographs for the book, on occasion raising himself from a warm and comfortable bed at unseemly hours to travel to Durham from Barnard Castle in order to capture, sometimes, just one moment in time. His wife, Christine, was frequently persuaded to accompany him on these expeditions. I can never fully express the gratitude I feel to them both for affording true friendship so unstintingly.

The Dean and Chapter of Durham have been wonderful. They have given information not available anywhere, save in the heads of those who daily tend the building which is Cuthbert's shrine.

The staff of Durham University Library, Palace Green, gave freely of their time to facilitate much research. The Master of University College, Durham, was most helpful with my efforts to ascertain the ownership of the Cuthbert Bede cartoons.

Nigel Cannaway of the Durham County Library Service sought out documents, some of which had not seen the light of day for many a long day. The archivists of Durham's County Hall, already under great pressure from their normal workload, made time to investigate my often strange research queries. My colleagues Patricia M. Cummins and Adrian Perrett of Macmillan College, Middlesbrough, Cleveland, have been an enormous help and have afforded me valuable assistance, primarily in retaining my sanity in moments when I thought this undertaking would never be completed.

I should also like to record my grateful thanks to the following for their help: Elizabeth Barker and her staff, Macmillan College Information Centre, Middlesbrough; The Manager and staff of the *Royal County Hotel*, Durham City; The Heritage Centre, the Bailey; St Nicholas' church, Market Place; St Oswald's church; John Shotton, antiquarian bookseller, Elvet Bridge; Tony Coia of Spennymoor; the staff of Harrison and Harrison, organ-builders.

The staff of Phillimore and Co. Ltd. deserve a very special mention for the loving care they have given to the production of this work.

There is also the lady and her cats who haunt the village whence some of my ancestors came. She knows who she is, what I owe to her, and that is sufficient.

Finally, I wish to acknowledge the debt I owe to my wife, Barbara, for the hours and days she has spent on her own while this book was conceived, written, and finally delivered. She proof-read the book, chapter by chapter; she always said it would never be finished; she was wrong again!

To the Reader

Apology

'I referre me wholly to the learned corrections of the Wise; for wel I wote that no treatise can allways be so workmanly handled but that somewhat sometymes may fall out amisse, contrarie to the expectation of the Reader: wherefore my petition to thee, Gentle Reader, is to accept these my travails with that minde I do offer them to Thee, and take gently that I give gladly; in so doing, I shall think my paines well bestowed, and shall bee encouraged hereafter to trust more to thy courtesie.'

Borrowed from M. A. Denham, Piercebridge, Darlington, 1846

Keith Proud, 1992

Introduction

The old expression remarks on an inability to see the wood for the trees, and this is certainly the case with Durham. The city is blessed with so many trees that they tend to be overlooked; they line the riverbank and fringe the roads, offering shade and greenery to Durham's every corner.

Durham's charm lies, arguably, in its infinite variety, in its superb blend of architectural styles from medieval to modern; in its ability to bewitch visitor and resident alike no matter what the weather, what the season, basking in brilliant sunshine or resplendent with silvered pavements after rain; multi-coloured autumn leaves fluttering onto its walkways and greens, preceding the first flurries of winter snow dusting the rooftops, gradually transforming the city into a fairytale Christmas land. Vegetable vendors in the ancient Market Place ply their frenzied trade while bankers, barristers and assorted undergraduates bustle about their business, brushing past ambling shoppers and tourists who linger, timeless, here and there, haunted by the beauty of the place.

I take enormous pride in the fact that I am one of Cuthbert's people, having known and loved the City of Durham for over 40 years. I was first brought here as a child, was later educated here and, although I admire many other European towns and cities and applaud their beauty and attractions, shall always maintain that none can compare with Durham's charm.

John Speed's 1610 map of the City of Durham carries the description:

> The ancient Citie Duram, by the Saxons called Dunholm, which as Beda sayth is compounded of their two words Dun, an hill and Holm an island, is in like form and situation as here is described. The first erectors of this Citie are sayde to be the Monks of Lindisferne which by the raging of the Danes were driven thence, and wandrig farre and wyde, at last by oracle (as in those dayes there were maney, if we believe their monkish legende) they were commanded to seat here, about the yere of grace 993 where Cuthbert their Bishop obtayned a great opinion of santitye and no less revenews and authoritye.
>
> In the upper part of this Citie, mounted upon an hill, William the Conqueror, for her defence built a strong Castell, and for her profitt and pleasure, nature hath girtt her almost round with ye sweet and delectable ryver of were.

There are, doubtless, many who would today take issue with Speed's description of the River Wear at Durham as 'sweet and delectable' and the monks actually arrived in 995, but the rest of the description will suffice.

An Anglo-Saxon poem describes Durham as a 'city celebrated in the whole Empire of the Britons'. Today that fame continues, and rightly so, but now visitors come from all parts of the world as well as from all over Britain. Many, it must be said, arrive with a totally false idea of what the city will be like.

They seem to expect a large church and castle surrounded as far as the eye can see by serried ranks of drab, Coronation Street-like terraces, a pall of industrial smoke enveloping all beneath it. Nothing could be further from the truth. Durham City is extremely beautiful, compact, charming to behold, fascinating and interesting in a myriad ways.

Cathedral, castle, university, ancient schools, bridges, an array of churches, an organ factory, a prison, a Market Place and some fine public buildings are the principal threads woven into the colourful tapestry which is the City of Durham today.

The first true builders of Durham were men of the Church, but they were not the first inhabitants. The large mound of Maiden Castle stands between Hallgarth Street and Shincliffe village, bearing testament to the existence of prehistoric inhabitants in the area, while at Old Durham, about a mile to the east of the Market Place, remains have been found of a Romano-British villa, occupied probably from the late second to the early fourth century. Some excavations in Durham City suggest that there were buildings on the peninsula before the monks arrived with St Cuthbert's body, and possibly as early as the Roman occupation of Britain; this should not be altogether

1. Durham Castle, from South Street.

Oliver Cromwell can be blamed for having consigned the Scottish prisoners to the cathedral and for other wrongs he and his followers inflicted on Durham City but, conversely, he also tried to institute what he saw as reforms. The powers of the bishops of Durham had once been vast but during the Commonwealth the See of Durham was dissolved. The Corporation of Durham bought the bishop's rights and privileges for a mere £200, but when Charles II was restored to England's throne even this paltry price was seen to have been a poor investment, for these rights were then lost.

It was also during Cromwell's time that the County of Durham first sent representatives to the House of Commons between the years 1653 and 1656. Attempts had been made to secure this right since the beginning of that century but, because of the power of the Bishop of Durham who so violently opposed the idea, nothing had previously been achieved. Now, with the bishop removed, the obstacle was gone. Henry Davison was the first member to represent the county, followed, in September 1654, by Robert and George Lilburn and James Clavering. The City of Durham was represented by Alderman Anthony Smith, a mercer, chosen by the freemen of the city.

Oliver Cromwell also succeeded, where many monarchs had tried and failed, in removing almost completely the power, influence and assets of the Bishop of Durham. It was a state of affairs destined not to be permanent but, while it existed, it condemned the bishop, Thomas Morton, to poverty, abuse and near oblivion. Almost in his stead there was created a parliamentary official, Sir Thomas Haselrig. He and his family bought prestigious property throughout the county, including the Bishop's Palace at Bishop Auckland which he remodelled to his own taste.

Thomas Morton was not the only Bishop of Durham to be treated harshly over the years and the main reason for this was that the power wielded by this office was both unique and immense.

These were powerful men, often referred to, somewhat inaccurately, as prince bishops, who, nevertheless, could be regarded almost as monarchs in their own right. They did owe allegiance to the sovereign but, because of the geographical position of their domain, the king realised full well the essential role they fulfilled as guardians of a buffer zone between his kingdom and that of the Scots. Many of Durham's bishops were an uneasy blend of the religious and the secular for, unlike their counterparts elsewhere in the land, they had to be of necessity, if not by inclination, part-churchman, part-soldier and part-politician, the precise degree of each constituent varying as time and circumstance dictated.

It was William I, the Conqueror, who first really appreciated the value to the monarchy of a powerful bishopric in the north. The very word 'bishopric' means 'the realm of the bishop' and Durham was precisely that, a realm stretching far beyond the present county's geographical and administrative boundaries. The Bishops of Durham of old held sway from the Tweed in the north to the Tees in the south, a situation which, for many reasons, suited successive rulers of England.

The Conqueror knew that he could safely tolerate the power and lifestyle enjoyed by the Bishop of Durham, a freedom he never could nor would have allowed to any of his lay barons. Under no circumstances imaginable would the bishop ever join forces with the Scots against his own sovereign, whereas a powerful secular noble might well have done so had the terms been favourable. The bishop was, in any case, far too busy defending his lands against the Scots and the dales bandits of Northumberland even to contemplate causing trouble for his king. Nor was the bishop himself ever likely to be easily usurped by a non-churchman, for the Bishopric of Durham could never have been ruled by a secular overlord. Custody of Cuthbert's body had been entrusted to the monks of Durham, and their leader, despite occasional 'minor' differences of opinion, was, undisputably, the bishop. As such, he could have no legal heirs to his see on his death and his successor was an appointee of the king. Were the see to fall vacant for a short time while the choice of a successor was considered, then all revenues from Durham accrued to the Crown.

Gradually, the power of the bishops increased to the point where they were practically omnipotent within their realm. The Bishop of Durham had his own courts, judges, army and even his own mint; proud to serve him were some of England's greatest nobles. His weapons were not only the rod and the staff but also the pen and the sword, a sword he was not afraid to wield when the occasion demanded forceful action.

Inevitably the time had to come, however, when Crown and Bishopric would come to blows, metaphorically if not actually; when Henry VIII called for the dissolution of the monasteries, he did not intend to spare Durham and its haughty lords. Cuthbert must, it seems, have continued the vigil over his last resting place because Durham suffered far less than most monasteries, as can be seen readily today.

During the bitter Civil War between King Charles I and the English Parliament, it was almost inevitable that the County of Durham, the intrinsic bishopric, should side with the king. The Puritans had no love for the established Church, nor for its bishops, and many of the people of the county and city were still all but espousing the old Roman Catholic religion, Puritanism being pure anathema to such folk who were loath to abandon the old ways. Even before the Civil War, in fact, the men of the majority of County Durham supported the king in his war against the Scots.

Charles I had first passed through the bishopric as a child when he followed his father, James VI of Scotland, James I of England, into his new kingdom. The royal children were then the guests of the Bishop of Durham at Auckland Castle. When, in 1633, Charles returned to the county, this time as king, he was entertained at Raby Castle near Staindrop and then again at Auckland Castle before riding in majesty into Durham City. The welcome prepared for him in 1633 was in marked contrast to that he was to receive 14 years later. On the former occasion he was met by the High Sheriff of Durham who was accompanied by an entourage of 200 men along with all the finest gentlemen of the county. Loyal greetings having been delivered, King Charles was accompanied by this great throng to the cathedral. Later that day he lodged at Durham Castle as the guest and at the expense of Bishop Morton, and a dear visit it proved to be, costing the churchman some £1,500 per day. On that occasion the king was on his way to be crowned in Edinburgh.

In February 1647, King Charles again passed through Durham but this time there were no welcoming gentlemen, for the king came as the prisoner of the English Parliament. He had been bought from the Scots for the sum of £20,000, a fee which also guaranteed the withdrawal of their army from English soil. The unhappy monarch travelled through the city on his way from Newcastle-upon-Tyne to London, closely guarded by Parliamentary commissioners.

Charles I eventually lost his head, and when his son, Charles II, was restored to the throne at the end of the Commonwealth, he did nothing to further the cause of a university for Durham. He did not plan to perpetuate a Cromwellian ideal.

During the 18th and 19th centuries, life in Durham City changed. No longer was it under constant threat of invasion. With this newfound stability, building began on a scale not seen in the city for hundreds of years. Graceful terraces rose where city walls had once stood as a necessity. The Baileys ceased to be places of safety and became instead fashionable addresses. Durham became a centre of justice with its law courts, a haven of culture with theatres and libraries; literature flourished, while the great and famous came to view and to grace the new order. The cathedral became a sort of Barchester where canons' wives seem, at times, to have wielded as much, if not more, power than the canons themselves. This was the Durham of polite society, a cultured place which attempted to emulate life in Bath or Cheltenham and, as far as can be ascertained, succeeded in that effort. Durham had no spa but neither Bath nor Cheltenham had Cuthbert.

3. View of Durham across the river.

In contrast to this way of life, there was also poverty, a scourge which was evident until the Second World War and even afterwards in parts. The miners who came to shop in Durham City must have looked into the windows of the stores and wondered how anyone could have afforded some items on display. There were slums in the city itself, some only recently demolished.

Today much of the city's population lives in pleasant suburbs, a lot of good, new housing having been erected since the 1950s. The old road pattern has altered almost beyond recognition.

Bridging the centuries as easily as its bridges span the river, this, then, is the City of Durham, last resting place of Cuthbert and of the Venerable Bede, one-time home of the notorious prince bishops of Durham and truly a city for all seasons.

Chapter One

Cuthbert – the Shepherd Saint

There was a time, several hundred years ago, when virtually every visitor to Durham was a pilgrim coming to do homage at the shrine of St Cuthbert. It is a somewhat sobering thought that many of today's visitors have never even heard of the man; as one tired American was overheard to say in the undercroft restaurant on being asked whether he had yet seen Cuthbert's tomb: 'Cuthbert who?'. Perhaps the time has come when, indeed, that very question should be asked. Who, after all, was this man, this monk of times long past, around whose miracles there arose a cult and on whose supposedly uncorrupt body the city of Durham was founded? A problem immediately presents itself, not because so little has been written about the man but because, on the contrary, so much has been written over so long a period of time that it is often extremely difficult to separate fact from fiction; the early writers were themselves confused, one going so far as to confuse Cuthbert with another saint and perhaps with more than one. There are, quite literally, hundreds of stories and legends about Cuthbert, so many that extracting evidence for their veracity is almost impossible. Suffice it to say that history has recorded some facts and people will believe what they wish about the saint, his miracles and the cult which arose after his death.

Cuthbert was probably born *c*.A.D. 634, many of the later monks of Durham believing that he was of royal Irish birth. It is probable that they were confusing Cuthbert's birth with that of St Molocus. The Venerable Bede, born during Cuthbert's lifetime and writing within 50 years of the saint's death, does not even refer to the man's birth nor to his earliest origins, starting his account of the life with boyhood in Scotland.

It must not be assumed that the north country into which Cuthbert came was a particularly civilised area. The Roman armies had finally left Britain at the start of the fifth century A.D. and a Romano-British land gradually became an English one. Christianity had already arrived in Britain but had not gained anything like a firm hold. It was Ireland where the faith was nurtured and grew in strength, and it was from there that missionaries were sent to Scotland to rekindle the light which had been extinguished on the mainland, as the Britons, Romano-Britons and incoming Anglo-Saxons worshipped the old pagan gods. Christian missionaries were also sent from Rome, Augustine arriving in Kent in A.D. 597, but it was the Irish who had the greatest impact in the north. Nevertheless it was the Roman missionary Paulinus who, in 627, at Easter, baptised Edwin as the first Christian King of Northumbria and went on to do the same to thousands of his subjects. Unfortunately, the new advent of Christianity in Northumbria was short-lived for many; Paulinus fled to the south in 633 when Edwin's army was defeated by the combined forces of Penda of Mercia and Cadwalla of Wales. Most of the northern people again reverted to the old religions.

By the time Edwin's second son, Oswald, regained the kingdom at the Battle of Heavenfield in 634, the year of Cuthbert's birth, much of Paulinus' work had been undone. It was into this age that Cuthbert was born, some would say fortuitously.

Most of the tales of Cuthbert's early life are set in southern Scotland, many of them near Melrose and in the Lammermuir Hills. One of the stories related about him as a boy describes how a younger boy rushed up to him in tears as they were playing and begged him to show more dignity. Such frivolous behaviour was not at all becoming to one who was destined to become a priest and, eventually, a bishop. Although Cuthbert did not understand the remark he comforted the youngster, who continued to protest the accuracy of his prophecy. On another occasion during his childhood, Cuthbert was visited, so the story goes, by an angel. For weeks Cuthbert had been suffering with a sore knee and was unable to rise from his bed, which had been placed outside the cottage so that he could enjoy the sunshine. He was roused from his sleep to discover that a stranger had approached on horseback. As was usual and customary at that time, Cuthbert offered the man hospitality. It was obvious to the stranger, however, that the boy could barely move. Dismounting from his horse,

4. View of Durham Abbey and adjoining scenery taken from the banks.

he examined Cuthbert's knee and suggested that he should apply to it a hot wheat poultice. This he did and a few days later was up and about, thanks to the advice of the angel, for surely that was what the horseman had been. It may be of interest to note that when the bones of Cuthbert were examined many centuries later at Durham Cathedral, it was noted that the man had once suffered from tuberculosis.

Another of the early stories demonstrates Cuthbert's courage, this incident occurring, it should be remembered, when most Northumbrians had reverted to paganism. A small group of monks was in a boat, behind which were several rafts loaded with timber. The journey was progressing well and their brothers in the monastery on the river-bank to the south were watching their approach. It was just then that a squall blew up, putting the monks on the river in great danger. People gathered on the north bank to enjoy their predicament, laughing and jeering at the men who claimed to worship the one true God. They were delighted, it seems, to see the monks in trouble. In the crowd was the young Cuthbert, who begged the Northumbrians to try to help the monks and to pray for their safety. The people jeered all the more and all Cuthbert could do in the midst of all this abuse was to fall on his knees in prayer. The wind changed, the waters became calm again and the monks landed safely on the south shore.

Some stories tell how Cuthbert was, at one point, a soldier, and others say that when he was about seventeen, in the year 651, he was a shepherd near the River Leader in the Lammermuir Hills. One night, as he kept vigil over his flock, he saw a band of angels guiding a soul up to heaven; a few days later, news was brought to the area that St Aidan had died. It was then, it is recorded, that Cuthbert decided to leave his sheep to become instead a shepherd of men by entering upon a religious life. Bidding farewell to his foster mother, Kenswith, he and a servant rode to the monastery at Melrose. As he approached and was handing his spear to the servant, out rushed Prior Boisil shouting, 'Behold the servant of the Lord'. Cuthbert was admitted to the order and stayed at Melrose for six or seven years. Then the abbot, Eata, was given a gift of more land, near Ripon, on which the king wished to see a new monastery built. A band of the Melrose monks, including Cuthbert, went off to start the work; he was to be guestmaster of the new foundation, it being his duty to ensure that all visitors to the monastery were treated hospitably and their needs met. Sadly, Eata soon afterwards fell from the king's favour and the monks returned to Melrose.

In 664, the year of the Synod of Whitby, at which it was decided that the English church would follow the ways of the Roman and not the Celtic Church, a plague struck the monastery at Melrose and caused devastation. Eata was by now Abbot of Lindisfarne, where he lived, as well as of Melrose but Boisil was still with Cuthbert at Melrose. These last were struck down, the other monks fearing for their safety, but Cuthbert recovered. Boisil was not so fortunate, and after a short period, during which he too predicted that Cuthbert would become a bishop, he died. The effects of the plague eventually over, Cuthbert tried to continue his work of teaching at the monastery but found the constraints of doing just that too much for him. He needed a new challenge and began to travel to villages away from Melrose, the more remote the better. Before long his reputation as a fine speaker preceded him and if there was not a large crowd when he arrived at a place, there was by the time he left. Cuthbert undoubtedly had what might today be called, somewhat simplistically perhaps, charisma.

As time passed, Cuthbert's journeys took him further and further away from his Melrose base so that he was absent from the monastery for weeks at a time. He must have suffered at times and he most certainly went short of food. Miraculous were the ways in which food is said to have been presented to him when none was available. On one occasion he found three pieces of dolphin meat by the sea shore; on another, when he was travelling with a young companion, they watched an eagle snatch a salmon from the river. When the bird dropped the fish, like piscine manna from heaven, Cuthbert insisted that the boy return half of the catch to the eagle before he would himself eat any of it.

On Cuthbert's journeys, he would occasionally visit religious houses like the priory at Coldingham, just to the north of Berwick. The abbess there, Ebba, sister to King Oswy, was one of his greatest friends. After this lady St Abb's Head, a stone's throw up the coast from Coldingham, takes its name. Cuthbert is often portrayed as a mysogynist, a hater of women, whereas he had, in fact, many female friends. On one of his visits to Coldingham, there was an incident which resulted in a story, with several variations, being handed down to posterity. Several times, Cuthbert, having waited until everyone else in the priory was asleep, rose from his bed and made his way to Coldingham shore, a beautiful expanse of sand even today. He waded out to the waist into the cold waves, praying and offering thanks to God for His kindness. As the dawn came up, he walked out of the sea and fell to his knees on the beach, at which point two otters, or seals, depending on which version of the tale is being related, also emerged from the waves, rubbing themselves against him to provide him with much-needed warmth after his nocturnal vigil. Unknown to Cuthbert, one of the monks from Coldingham had watched all night from the higher ground, suspicious of Cuthbert's movements. Why, after all, was he abroad when the rest of the community was asleep? Later the next day he confessed to Cuthbert what he had done and begged forgiveness for doubting the man from Melrose. This Cuthbert readily granted, but instructed him to reveal nothing of what he had seen until he, Cuthbert, had died.

Cuthbert lived and worked for 13 years at Melrose and then Eata asked him to become Prior of Lindisfarne, so he went to the remote Northumbrian outpost, teaching the monks the new way of monastic life decreed by the Synod of Whitby. These were not only the rules set down by a monk called Benedict who had lived, in Italy, 200 years before Cuthbert, but also those of Columba. Obedience, poverty and chastity were the tenets which Benedict had decreed to be the essentials of a Christian monastic life, while Columba's were even more strict. Not unnaturally, the monks of this semi-island did not like the new rules and daily argued against them at the meeting of the chapter. Cuthbert sometimes argued his case but, if he tired of the controversy, he never lost his temper but simply retired from the meeting. On his return to the forum the next day, he behaved as if there had never been any dissension, explaining anew his reasons for wishing the community to adopt the new regime. At last he won the day, and the monks accepted his will. There was, after all, something to be said for a way of life which produced a man of the character of Cuthbert; why was it, they asked themselves, that he never lost his temper and was always cheerful, even under the most extreme pressure? Cuthbert himself had one seemingly insoluble problem; he was unable to settle for long in one place. His attempted solution was to leave Lindisfarne at low tide and to travel about the mainland preaching in the nearby villages. He seemed to know, however, that this was not his destiny.

While Cuthbert was Prior of Lindisfarne, Britain, in 668, acquired its first archbishop, a Greek called Theodore. Eata, though still based on Lindisfarne, became Bishop of northern Northumbria. Whether or not these changes caused the hiatus in Cuthbert's life will never be known but he suddenly felt the need for the sort of solitude which could be found only on distant places like the Farne Islands, a group of scattered, sparsely-vegetated, black rocks lying just off the coast of Northumberland. After 12 years as Prior of Lindisfarne, in a desire to be even nearer to God, Cuthbert, like Aidan before him, sought the solitude of the islands.

The island nearest to the mainland is Inner Farne, some 16 acres in extent, barren and with little grass or vegetation; even in Cuthbert's day, however, it was a haven for tens of thousands of seabirds. This was where Cuthbert decided to settle. When he arrived on the island, he was beset by demons, it is said, but he drove away these 'evil spirits' and set about the serious business of creating for himself a shelter. Not only did he erect a hut in which to live but he also busied himself with creating another which was dedicated to prayer. His materials were nothing but stones and soil, and surrounding the two huts Cuthbert built a wall, so high that all he could see from within was the sky.

One of the most serious problems Cuthbert had was finding a supply of drinking water in this inhospitable place, but help was to hand from his friends on Lindisfarne. They rowed across to Inner Farne and dug a well inside his high wall, Cuthbert praying that water would be found. His prayers were answered. The Lindisfarne monks also helped in the building of a house for the many visitors who came to see Cuthbert. For some time, all of his food was rowed across from Lindisfarne but Cuthbert wanted to be more self-sufficient. He cultivated a patch of ground into which he sowed wheat seed. The crop failed. The following year he planted barley and that was successful.

During these three years on the island, Cuthbert had many visitors, all of whom he greeted in the guest house, allowing nobody inside his wall. He became increasingly reclusive, greeting visitors only through a hole in the wall, which was also used to pass food to him once he had ceased to tend his crops.

There was one occasion when Cuthbert left the island and that was to travel not to Lindisfarne but to Coquet Island, some way down the Northumbrian coast. He made the journey to meet his friend Elfled, Abbess of Whitby, Coquet Island having been selected as a convenient venue since neither felt able to journey the full distance. At this meeting Cuthbert again expressed his concern that he would soon be called upon to become a bishop, but not long afterwards the call came.

In 685, at a meeting of Church leaders, Cuthbert was chosen to become Bishop of Hexham, but when the news was brought to him he practically ignored the

5. Stained-glass window depicting St Cuthbert, west wall of Durham Cathedral.

messengers and their letters. For weeks he prevaricated until the situation demanded forthright action. The king himself, with a large band of important retainers and Churchmen, sailed from the Northumbrian coast to Cuthbert's island. On this occasion, Cuthbert came out from behind his walls to meet his visitors. As he approached, they fell to their knees, beseeching him to submit to the request he had so long dreaded. Although he did, eventually, agree to their wishes, he managed to avoid taking up his appointment for several months and when he did become a bishop he refused to wear anything other than his simple monk's robes. Hexham was a long way from the Farnes but Eata asked him to come to Melrose. It was agreed there that he, Eata, would take the bishopric of Hexham in order that Cuthbert could be Bishop of Lindisfarne in his stead. Cuthbert undertook the duties required of him as a bishop but still found time to travel to the loneliest outposts of the area to preach the word of God.

Cuthbert was 51 when he had a premonition that death was near. He had been bishop for just two years when he resigned the office and returned to Inner Farne. Now, however, he was not so much of a recluse. When the monks visited him from Lindisfarne, he emerged to talk to them but, after two months, he became ill. The Abbot of Lindisfarne, Herefrith, crossed the short stretch of water to beg him to return to the comparative comfort of the Holy Island but Cuthbert would have none of it. He told Herefrith that nearby, when the time was right, would be found a coffin in which he wished to be buried. Herefrith returned with the news to the monastery, where for five days he led the monks in prayer for Cuthbert. When a party of monks crossed again to Inner Farne, they found Cuthbert waiting for them in the little guest house; in all that time he had eaten just half an onion. He asked to be helped back to his own hut where, very soon afterwards, he died.

Cuthbert had wanted to be buried on Inner Farne but the monks begged that his resting place should be on Lindisfarne. He allowed them to have their way but only on condition that if ever Lindisfarne and its monastic life were threatened they would take his bones with them if they had to flee. The body was washed and wrapped first in linen and then a wax cloth, to preserve it before being moved to the monastery. It was then rowed back to Holy Island where it was buried in a stone coffin to the right of the altar in the monastery church. The year was 687.

Chapter Two

The Cuthbert Cult

Dead Cuthbert certainly was, but he was not forgotten. Stories soon began to circulate about people who were cured of their ailments simply by visiting his burial place; naturally, more and more people came to see if the saint could reach from beyond the grave to help them.

It was not unusual at that time for an important person's bones to be exhumed, washed and reburied, wrapped in expensive fabric. Some 11 years after Cuthbert's death, in 698, the monks decided to accord him this honour. When they uncovered and opened the coffin, however, they were amazed to find the body looking as it must have done at death. Cuthbert looked, they reported, as if he were simply asleep. Having made their findings known to their bishop, they disturbed as little as possible and placed the body in a new coffin. This time it was kept above ground.

Still Lindisfarne continued to be visited by pilgrims, now greater in number than before, but in 793 the island had its first taste of some very unwelcome visitors. These were Danish Vikings who ransacked the church and killed some of the monks. In 794 there was another Viking raid, this time so great that the monks fled for their lives, leaving behind Cuthbert's body. When they returned they found that, although the rest of their treasures had gone, Cuthbert's tomb had not been touched.

There was then a long period of comparative peace until in 875 the Danish raiders returned. The monks again had no choice but to leave Lindisfarne, and they took with them not only St Cuthbert and his coffin but also some other precious relics, the head of King Oswald, some of St Aidan's bones and those of Eata. Several of the islanders heard that the monks were leaving and joined their train. Although they may have guessed that they might be absent from Lindisfarne for some time, the monks could not have foreseen that they were destined to travel about with the coffin for seven long years, resting in so many places before settling first at Chester-le-Street and then at Durham. Wherever they arrived with the cart bearing the coffin and other relics, they were met with kindness and, often, with gifts. Cuthbert's fame, in life and death, had reached into even the most remote fastnesses of the area. However large the saint's retinue, and numbers must have fluctuated over the years, only seven of the monks were allowed to touch the coffin, or shrine, and the cart on which it was transported. At a later date, a horse was provided to relieve the monks of all the pushing and pulling.

John de Wessington, Prior of Durham in the early 15th century and a gifted scholar, compiled an itinerary of the places he thought had been visited by the guardians of Cuthbert's shrine, his careful research based largely on churches dedicated to St Cuthbert. In Northumberland he found six, in Westmorland one, in Cumberland four, in Lancashire eleven. Yorkshire had three, Richmondshire five, Cleveland seven, and in Durham there were four. In the early 19th century James

6. Wall painting of a bishop, Galilee chapel, Durham Cathedral.

Raine, historian and friend of Robert Surtees, and editor of the fourth volume of that writer's monumental *History of Durham*, consulted Wessington's research and reconstructed what he considered to be the route taken by Cuthbert's guardians. Having left the island, they went to Doddington, Elsdon, Bellingham, Haydon Bridge and then along the course of the South Tyne to Beltingham. This was followed by a journey along part of Hadrian's Wall and so to Bewcastle and Carlisle. Salkeld was the next halt then Edenhall and on to Plumbland. Burnsall, Middleton, Halsall, Lytham, Hambledon, Kellet, Furness, Aldingham, Kirkby Ireleth and Hawkshead took them on a convoluted loop into the Lake District.

Still they did not feel safe and must have recalled the promise given to Cuthbert by his brother monks that his remains would be safeguarded, for they considered that they would be well-advised to cross to Ireland. They made their way to Workington where a ship was readied, the body and treasures put aboard and, with many monks left on the bank, space being very limited, the vessel sailed. It did not, however, go very far; a storm arose of such ferocity that the monks rapidly concluded when it ceased that Cuthbert had no desire to be transported to the Emerald Isle. They returned whence they had come.

It was during this storm, it is recorded, that their jewel-adorned volume of the Lindisfarne Gospels was lost overboard. When it was learned that the book had miraculously turned up at Whithorn, home some 500 years earlier of St Ninian who had there founded Candida Casa, a Christian church and school, the Cuthbert procession headed north. There is, perhaps, something fatalistic and touching in the fact that Candida Casa means 'white church', and that the first great Saxon House of God in Durham was known as the White Church. Their book retrieved, the monks went across the bleak Pennines via Cliburn and Dufton down Teesdale, stopping, it could be argued, at Cotherstone, then on to Marske near Richmond, to Forcett and South Cowton. The next stage took them through Barton, Overton, Fishlake and Ackworth before a huge stride north-east to Kildale, Middleton, Marton, Ormesby, Wilton and Kirkleatham, as if they were heading for the vast mouth of the River Tees. Certainly they would find no easy crossing point there. Back they moved, inland to Redmarshall, near the modern Stockton, and north to Chester-le-Street, the old Roman station.

After a sojourn there of 113 years and the passage of several generations of monks, the guardians were forced, by renewed Danish activity, to speed south to Ripon. Their stay there was brief indeed and it was while attempting to return to Chester-le-Street that the spirit of St Cuthbert refused to allow them to pass the place which was to become Durham. The man who had led the monks and their treasures south to Ripon was Bishop Aldhun, the last true guardian of Chester-le-Street, and the monk destined to become the first Bishop of Durham. He had, in his younger days, been tutor to King Edward the Confessor.

There are numerous stories of how Durham came to be selected but they all revolve around a lost cow and either one or two women. As the monks were at Wrdelau (Warden Law?), a hill between Houghton-le-Spring and the coastal village of Seaham, which itself has Cuthbertian connections, they found that they were unable to move the cart carrying the shrine. It remained immovable for three days during which time one of the monks, Eadmer, had a vision of St Cuthbert in which he was told that the remains were to be taken to Dunholme. This information he relayed to the rest of the party; the problem was that nobody knew where this Dunholme was. It was then that two young girls passed the place where the cart was stuck. One was asking the other if she had seen her lost cow, a brown animal. She most certainly had; it was across at Dunholme. It had strayed a long way from Warden Law! As the monks set off to find Dunholme, the cart moved easily

7.   The dun cow panel, cathedral north wall.

and it was not long before they arrived at this appointed place, a piece of high ground surrounded by a great loop in the River Wear. The site was 'strong by nature, but not easily rendered habitable, as it was overgrown by a thick forest. In the midst was a small plain, which had been used in tillage'. Once the word was put about that Cuthbert's remains were at a new home, people travelled from all parts of the area to help the monks in the business of clearing the site. The first job for Cuthbert's guardians was to erect a shelter for the shrine, 'a little church built quickly of rods'. Next they built a more permanent wooden church.

On 4 September 999, just four years after their arrival at Durham, Aldhun dedicated a large stone church into which Cuthbert's remains were placed. This 'White Church', complete at the time except for its western tower, was cruciform in plan and was designed to have either two or three towers. John Sykes records in his *Local Records* that the White Church had two towers, a central tower and another at the west end, with brass-covered pinnacles. Quite when the western tower was completed is not clear.

As time passed, yet more relics were deposited at Durham, drawing greater numbers of pilgrims. Early in the 11th century a priest called Elfrid, sacrist to the monastery and sometime guardian of Cuthbert's body, became convinced that it was God's will that he should travel all over Northumbria collecting, some would say stealing, the remains of holy people buried there. During his quest he stole the remains of two hermits, two Bishops of Hexham, two abbesses and a king. He even removed the bones of St Boisil from Melrose. There was, however, one set of remains which remained elusive and they were at Jarrow where, it must be supposed, the monks knew of his ways. For several years he was thwarted in his attempts to procure the bones of the Venerable Bede but in about 1020, after days spent there in prayer and meditation, he left Jarrow, never to return, but the long vigil was over for Elfrid in more ways than one. He carried with him the saint's bones which were deposited at Durham. It was not until after Elfrid's death, however, that the precise location of Bede's bones was discovered. He had placed them in the coffin with the body of Cuthbert. Nor, yet, was Cuthbert himself to be allowed to rest in peace. The Vikings were no longer a scourge; in fact the great King Canute travelled barefoot to Durham to heap honour on him, but close relatives of the Vikings, the Normans, were soon to cause more upheaval for Cuthbert and the Durham monks.

In 1069, just three years after the Battle of Hastings, King William I became concerned when some of the northern earls and Ethelwin, Bishop of Durham, led a rebellion against him. Once it was put down, he created Robert Cumyn, one of his nobles, Earl of Northumberland. When, a short time later, he and all of his soldiers but one were butchered by the men of Durham, William marched north to extract vengeance.

When Ethelwin and the monks heard of the king's intentions, they took their sacred relics, including Cuthbert's body, and set off towards Lindisfarne by way of Jarrow and Bedlington. When, on the fourth day, they stood on the shore opposite the island, they were unable to cross because the tide was in and passage is only possible at low tide. Had they forgotten this after so long an absence from the place? In their view, another Cuthbert miracle intervened, the saint's body taking on this time the role of a latter-day Moses. The waters receded, allowing the monks to cross to safety, covering the way again as soon as the last of the party was over. After four months on Holy Island, the monks returned the body to Durham but found that William had laid waste the countryside between Durham and York, destroying crops, houses and churches as well as slaughtering people indiscriminately. The land he left behind was a famine-ridden desert. Still, Cuthbert was home again. The mystery surrounding the uncorruptibility of Cuthbert's body was to linger on for centuries.

In 1104, when the new Norman cathedral was considered ready to receive the body which had been resting for some time in a stone tomb in the cloister garth, the decision was taken to examine the remains again before they were placed in the new tomb behind the high altar. The examination was to be carried out at night by the prior and nine monks who began their task, with all due ceremony, on 29 August. Having broken open the coffin lid, they found inside a perfectly preserved oak coffin. They moved the coffin into the middle of the choir, and on opening it found a linen cloth beneath which lay the body of St Cuthbert looking more asleep than dead. He was lying on his right side. A sweet smell emerged from the coffin, suggesting that the body had been embalmed many centuries earlier. Also in the coffin were various treasures, relics of other saints and, in a small sack, the bones of Bede. The monks found, on removing the body, that it bent in the middle. Some relics were removed from the coffin into which the body was then replaced, and the whole was moved back to the shrine. It was soon afterwards removed again so that Cuthbert's body could be wrapped in expensive cloth.

Durham was being visited at the time by many important Church dignitaries, so important was the moving of the saint's body considered to be. Some of them expressed serious concern about the secretive way in which the monks had just carried out their examination of the body, going so far as to suggest that it was nothing more than a collection of bones, or perhaps they thought it was an actor feigning death. Yet another examination was agreed, therefore, and this time there were about fifty people present. Out came the coffin again.

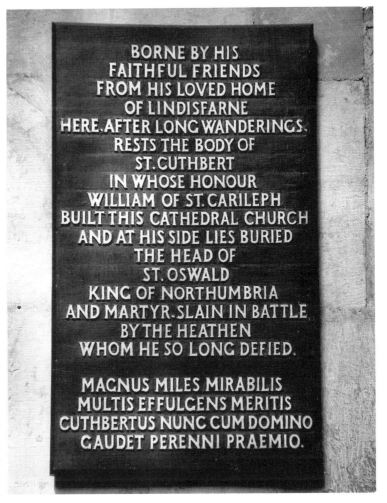

8.   Explanation of St Cuthbert's tomb, Durham Cathedral.

The examiner was a visiting abbot who lifted Cuthbert's head, moved it about and pulled the ears before he was satisfied. The gathering concluded, after witnessing this exhibition, that Cuthbert was dead and that the body was uncorrupt.

In the 16th century, as part of the Dissolution of the Monasteries, three commissioners of King Henry VIII arrived in Durham to remove the treasures of the cathedral. Suspecting that there might be something of value in Cuthbert's shrine they had it broken open, but the workman charged with the job accidentally broke open the coffin, breaking one of Cuthbert's legs. He saw quite easily that there was a complete body inside, the face sporting a beard. Two of the commissioners were called to see this for themselves. They had the body removed to a nearby vestry and

9. St Cuthbert's pectoral cross.

waited to hear what the king wanted to have done with it. When nothing was heard from Henry, the bishop had the body reburied behind the high altar beneath a slab of blue marble.

Almost 300 years later, in 1827, several men of influence at the cathedral opened the tomb again. The dean and chapter librarian, James Raine, the man responsible for researching the route of the body's travels in the 10th century, recorded the happenings. The blue marble slab having been removed, the workmen encountered almost two feet of soil beneath which was another stone slab. That put to one side, there was revealed a pit some four feet deep, at the bottom of which was a large, but badly decaying, oak coffin. Within it was another, in an even worse state of preservation. After a motley collection of human bones had been removed a third coffin was found, the most decayed of all. After investigation the examiners concluded that this was the coffin which had been opened in 1104. Within it was a skeleton, wrapped in five layers of clothes. Secreted deep in this fabric was the wonderful pectoral cross, probably Cuthbert's own, now so well known as a symbol of Durham. This, together with a comb, a portable altar, some clothing and pieces of the original coffin were removed and displayed first in the dean and chapter library, then in a special room in the cathedral undercroft. The stole and maniple found in the coffin had originally been ordered to be made by Queen Elfleda for the Bishop of Winchester. Two years after this prelate's death, they were brought to Chester-le-Street as an offering at Cuthbert's shrine by King Athelstan. At the end of the examination all the human remains were reburied on the site in a new coffin.

There was to be yet another opening of the coffin. In 1889 it was confirmed that the skeleton contained in the grave was almost certainly that of Cuthbert. The bones were still covered in a membrane, again suggestive of early embalming. A missing shinbone tallied with the breaking of one of Cuthbert's legs by the workman during the 16th century.

There is a strange legend which surfaces from time to time around the cathedral, a ghost which will not be laid. Soon after Queen Elizabeth I, a Protestant, came to the throne a small band of monks still adhering to Roman Catholicism broke into Cuthbert's tomb and removed his body. This was then hidden by three of them in another part of the cathedral. When one of the three Benedictine monks died the other two entrusted another with the secret, which has thus been passed down to the present day. Most historians shrug this off as a fairy story, but some people believe that the tomb could have been entered from the Chapel of the Nine Altars, part of the cathedral which is built on a lower level than that occupied by Cuthbert's grave.

What is even more of a mystery than this legend and the uncorruptibility of Cuthbert's body is the comparatively modern find of the pectoral cross. That it is genuine and 'right' is beyond all doubt, but in all the investigations of the body and its clothing, how was it missed so many times? Perhaps it was found on earlier examinations and just quietly replaced in its hiding place. Today it is still safe, and one of the greatest treasures of not only Durham Cathedral but of the whole of the Christian world and faith.

Chapter Three

Durham Cathedral

Durham Cathedral is, by any standards, an architectural masterpiece. It is also a magnificent tribute to those who conceived and built it, knowing full well that they would never witness the complete fruition of their labours but demonstrating their unswerving faith in the future. To these men Durham owes a great debt.

The cathedral was not the first building on Durham's peninsula erected to house the remains of St Cuthbert nor is it exactly as its Norman builders first conceived it. Over the centuries there have been some modifications and repairs to the building started by Bishop William of St Calais (St Carileph) in 1092. Compared to its

10. Romantic Victorian view of Durham Cathedral and Castle.

26

contemporaries, however, Durham has been altered little and remains one of the finest-ever examples of architectural innovation.

The earliest mention of Christianity in the area now known as Durham City occurs in the *Anglo-Saxon Chronicle*, which records that on 17 July 762, a priest called Peohtwine was consecrated Bishop of Whithorn, in Galloway, at Aelfet ee, translated as 'Elvet Island'. This 'island' was in all probability the peninsula of Durham or somewhere in the area known as Elvet, possibly near the present St Oswald's church. It was more than 200 years later, in A.D. 995, that the man known to history as the first Bishop of Durham, Aldhun, settled on the peninsula with his monks and their followers, together with the precious relics of St Cuthbert.

Most visitors to Durham Cathedral approach, as they have done for centuries, along Saddler Street and up narrow Owengate to emerge on Palace Green, a vast grass rectangle separating cathedral from castle and bordered on two sides by a beautiful range of buildings. From the top of Owengate, the first sight of this awesome and beautiful cathedral is unforgettable, nor does the sensation diminish on subsequent visits. The sheer size of the place, a vastness enhanced because it is not, like York for example, surrounded by other buildings, is difficult to absorb. Everything about it is massive but in perfect proportion. The great nave runs for 201 ft., its roof vault rising some 72 ft., while the choir is 132 ft. long. The magnificent central tower climbs for a phenomenal 218 ft. The entire building stretches 470 ft. from the east wall of the Chapel of the Nine Altars to the west wall of the Galilee chapel, and its builders really do seem to have been reaching for heaven; the pinnacles of the twin western towers point the way and echo the desire. The work of building this great House of God is ascribed to several distinct periods. Work on the nave, transepts and the four west choir bays took place from 1093 to 1133, and Bishop Hugh Pudsey added the Galilee chapel at the west end in 1175; the west towers were built between 1217 and 1226, while between 1242 and 1280 the east end of the choir was altered and the Chapel of the Nine Altars erected. The great central tower was rebuilt between 1465 and 1495.

The first Norman Bishop of Durham, Walcher, wanted to see sweeping changes in the north. He was King William's man, from Lorraine, and was determined to stamp William's authority on the church at Durham. The old White Church was administered by secular priests who were often indistinguishable from common people. They took wives, had children and lived largely as they wished. Bishop Walcher allowed a group of Benedictine monks to come north and to settle in the ruins of the church at Jarrow, his ultimate aim being to oust the Saxon priests from Durham and to replace them with the Benedictines. This plan was delayed when Bishop Walcher was murdered by a mob at Gateshead in 1080. It was left to his successor, William of St Calais, or St Carileph, to implement the Benedictine move. This he did, having applied to the Pope for proper permission to set up the new order at Durham. The celibate Benedictine monks were installed, but the secular monks were not simply evicted; those who were prepared to embrace the new order were told that they could remain, although only one did so. The rest were dispersed to new homes at Norton, Darlington and St Andrew's Auckland.

11.   An engraving of 1841 by R. W. Billings showing the north aisle of the cathedral, looking east.

The White Church at Durham was another Saxon remnant, not nearly grand enough a repository for Cuthbert's remains and the Normans decided that this too had to go. It was at this point that Bishop St Calais became involved in a plot against the Conqueror's successor, William Rufus, and when this was discovered in 1088 St Calais retreated to sanctuary in Normandy. Seeing the new churches which were being built there he returned to Durham in 1091 having received the royal pardon and fired with enthusiasm for the new architectural ideas. In 1092, St Calais ordered

12. A Billings engraving of 1841 showing the south doorway of the cathedral, leading into the cloisters.

the demolition of the White Church and a year later, on 11 August 1093, the foundation stones for the new monastic church were laid. Malcolm, King of Scotland was present. The arrangement St Calais had with the Durham monks was that if they funded the erection of the new monastic buildings he would provide the money for the church. When he died in 1096, the monks decided that the church should remain a priority and diverted their finance to it. In 1099 Ralph Flambard became the new Bishop of Durham, by which time the nave had been built.

13.   Interior of the Galilee chapel, Durham Cathedral.

Flambard also had to flee across the Channel, having escaped from the Tower of London in which he had been incarcerated by the new monarch, Henry I. In Normandy he plotted against Henry, and was one of the leaders of an intended invasion of England. After receiving his pardon, he went to Durham where, as well as founding Kepier hospital and giving Finchale Hermitage to the monks, he continued work on the monastery and church, carrying the walls to the height of the roof. He also created Palace Green and ordered the building of Framwellgate Bridge. It was during Flambard's episcopacy, on 4 September 1104, that St Cuthbert's remains were removed from their temporary cloister home and placed with great ceremony in 'a goodly sepulchre prepared for that purpose' in the new church.

It was to be five years before a new bishop was appointed and during 1128-33 the monks finished their church. Bishop Geoffrey Rufus built the great north and south doorways of the nave and constructed for the monastery a wonderful chapter house, said to have been the finest in England until it was rebuilt by the Victorians in 1895. Geoffrey Rufus was buried there in 1140.

One of the most powerful of the Durham bishops was Hugh Pudsey, just in his mid-20s when he was elected in 1153. Although he did not always get on well with the monks this was by no means unusual. Pudsey provided for Finchale to become a priory, and also built a hospital for 65 lepers at Sherburn. Two more were built at Northallerton and Witton Gilbert, while the Norman Gallery in Durham Castle and also Elvet Bridge were constructed at his instigation.

Pudsey's contribution to the church at Durham was significant. At first he considered adding to the structure's east end, but several accidents hindered progress so

14.   A Billings engraving of 1841 showing the east walk of the cloisters.

significantly that the bishop concluded that God did not want changes there. Abandoning that idea, Pudsey looked to the other end of the church and built the Galilee chapel. Before this was created, the main entrance to the church had been through massive western doors, which Pudsey replaced with a new entrance on the north side. Pudsey's architects and builders did not have much space in which to work, there being little land at what was formerly the west end of the church. The chapel is, consequently, very wide in comparison to its length. Built on solid rock, it is felt by many to be the best example in England of Transitional Norman/Early English architecture. Although Pudsey was a builder of graceful structures, their foundations were not always as they should have been, and considerable repairs have been necessary through the years.

As well as this extensive architectural legacy, Pudsey created the Boldon Book, an enormous survey of the palatinate's holdings undertaken in 1183 and covering the

15.   Sanctuary knocker, north door of cathedral.

area which had been omitted almost 100 years before. The survey was made at a time when the See was consolidating its power and the expense of many of the kind's rights. It was to be used in the bishop's exchequer and listed the money and labour dues owed to the bishop by his estates.

Richard le Poore became Bishop of Durham in 1228, moving from Salisbury, whose cathedral he had just built. When he first saw the church at Durham, the east end was made up of three semi-circular apses, the central one apsidal inside and out, the two others apses within and rectangles outside. Ignoring Pudsey's failure to build there, he conceived the idea of the Chapel of the Nine Altars although building was not started until after his death; it was then designed and erected by the prior, Thomas of Melsonby. It was this Thomas who also oversaw the building of the central tower to the height of the gallery, the complete operation taking another quarter of a century.

In the very early years of the 15th century, Bishop Walter Skirlaw paid for a great deal of the basic laying out and essential construction work of the monastery cloisters attached to the church, but it was his successor, Thomas Langley, the last of the great medieval prince bishops, who almost completed them. He also constructed a fountain there, protecting its users from the elements with an elaborate octagonal surround. Bishop Langley also repaired Pudsey's Galilee chapel, which was in serious danger of slipping from its foundations into the River Wear.

It was in 1429 that Prior John de Wessington, a member of the family from which George Washington was descended, wrote to Bishop Langley giving details of the great storm and resultant fire which had destroyed the great central tower of the monastic church overnight. Repairs were put in hand but were purely temporary. By 1456 the tower was in such a sorry state that the prior informed Bishop Neville of his fears every time there was a storm. Proper repairs were still not begun until 1470 and that at only the lower levels; the upper stage was added between 1484-94. There have, of course, been other minor alterations and repairs to the cathedral over the centuries and some acts of gross vandalism too.

The main entrance to Durham Cathedral is the great north door. To this was affixed the sanctuary knocker, a criminal's hope of salvation, for it was here that fugitives could find temporary shelter and immunity from prosecution even though their pursuers might be at their very heels. It was not, in fact, necessary for the pursued to grasp the knocker because the boundaries of sanctuary at Durham extended well away from the church, probably as far as Neville's Cross and Gilesgate. It should be noted here that the sanctuary knocker in place today is a replica of the original. It is a Romanesque bronze piece, taking the form of a lion's head, its mane spread, and measuring 22 ins. deep. The eye sockets may once have held coloured enamel. There is still uncertainty as to the knocker's precise age, and it is argued that while it was probably originally placed in its present position in the 1150s when Bishop Pudsey created the north porch, it could well have had an earlier home elsewhere on the site.

The English right of sanctuary can be traced back to 597 when the laws of King Ethelbert of Kent decreed that those who violated the peace of the church would be punished. Later Saxon laws continued the practice, even giving such places as Durham, which was held in high regard because of its Cuthbertian links, special privileges of sanctuary. The Normans continued to observe the tradition. At Durham, sanctuary was granted for 37 days. A fugitive would knock on the door, and then would be admitted to the church, only if he were carrying no weapons, by one of the watchers who kept vigil in a small room over the north porch. This room no longer exists. He would then be taken to a grilled alcove where he was given bedding and food. The watcher who had admitted him then tolled the Galilee bell to inform the world outside that a fugitive had been taken in. The prior was then given what details were available about the felon. One of the main reasons why Durham was so popular as a place of sanctuary, some runaways travelling there from as far away as Somerset and Surrey, was that it had its own Palatine coroner who could resolve matters quickly. When he arrived, he heard the man's confession at St Cuthbert's shrine. The fugitive then had to swear an oath promising that he would leave the country as quickly as possible, travelling to a port to seek passage abroad. Should he have failed to find this within 40 days, he had to return to sanctuary. An act passed during the reign of Henry VIII also required the coroner to witness the branding of the letter 'A' with a hot iron on the flat of the man's right thumb.

While in sanctuary, the fugitive was made to wear a black gown with a large yellow cross of St Cuthbert on the left shoulder. He was able to attend services and wander about the church. Had he the ways and means, he was also allowed to conclude any business he had left unfinished. Towards the end of the allotted 37 days the man was directed to, or chose, a port to which he travelled wearing only a single piece of sackcloth clothing and carrying a white wooden cross. The law protected him from being abused as he made his way there. Efforts to end the right of sanctuary, for many and various reasons, were made as early as 1531. Queen Mary attempted to reinstate it, but Elizabeth I hastened it on its way and in 1624 the entire system was abolished by King James I.

16.   Detail of carving on arches, Galilee chapel, Durham Cathedral.

On entering the cathedral, the visitor cannot help but notice the immediate sense of space, a sensation enhanced by the great height of the rib-vaulted stone roof supported on gigantic pillars. Nor is Durham Cathedral cluttered with the multitude of effigies and tombs so often encountered in other great churches. There are tombs and memorials but not in any number and always unobtrusive. One of the reasons for this is that, because of the great sanctity of Cuthbert, not even bishops were initially allowed burial in the church, although this convention was sometimes ignored in later times. The interior of the cathedral is not precisely as it was before the Reformation and the later vandalism of thousands of imprisoned Scots. A rood screen which used to stand between the two pillars at the east end of the nave was destroyed during the Reformation, along with some 30 altars in various parts of the church.

The carved wooden font canopy, in the area between the north and south door, dates from the 17th century and was probably designed by James Clement, a Durham architect. It is contemporary with the stalls and canopies in the choir, some of which are also ascribed to Clement. It was during the episcopacy of John Cosin, that great lover of wood, that much restoration of the cathedral furniture was undertaken. Just to the east of the font a marble line set into the floor indicates the point beyond

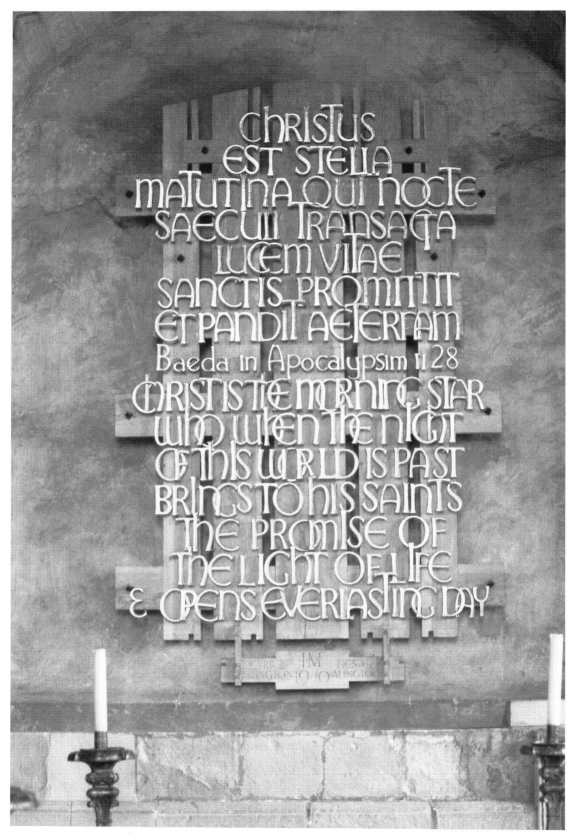

CHRISTUS
EST STELLA
MATUTINA QUI NOCTE
SAECULI TRANSACTA
LUCEM VITAE
SANCTIS PROMITTIT
ET PANDIT AETERNAM

Baeda in Apocalypsim ii 28

CHRIST IS THE MORNING STAR
WHO WHEN THE NIGHT
OF THIS WORLD IS PAST
BRINGS TO HIS SAINTS
THE PROMISE OF
THE LIGHT OF LIFE
& OPENS EVERLASTING DAY

17.   Inscription in Galilee chapel, Durham Cathedral.

which, under Benedictine rules, no woman was allowed to pass. This was the closest they could approach to Cuthbert's shrine.

The cathedral abounds in fascinating stories. In the Galilee chapel is the simple tomb of the Venerable Bede. When Bede's bones were first brought to Durham they were hidden in Cuthbert's tomb, but in the 12th century Bishop Pudsey had them removed and placed in a jewelled silver-gilt shrine. They were moved to the Galilee chapel in 1370. The tomb holds the remains of England's first true historian, and the inscription it carries reads 'HAC SUNT IN FOSSA BEDAE VENERABILIS OSSA'. Legend tells that the man carving the inscription fell asleep, having intended to chisel '... BEDAE SANCTI OSSA'. When he awoke he found that the work had been done for him, supposedly by an angel, and a literary one at that.

In the nave, a little to the east of the miners' memorial, are the tombs of some members of the once-powerful Neville family, of Raby Castle near Staindrop. They have strong connections with the cathedral, were the first lay people to be buried in it and gave money to beautify it. The more easterly tomb is that of the victor of the Battle of Neville's Cross, Ralph, 4th Baron Neville. To the west is the last resting place of his son John, 5th Baron Neville, who, in 1372, presented 200 pounds of silver to purchase a new base for St Cuthbert's shrine and 500 marks towards the cost of a screen, the beautiful Neville Screen, behind the high altar. He was with his father at Neville's Cross. Both men's wives also appear in effigy, Lord John having been married to Maud, daughter of the famed Harry Hotspur. These tombs were badly damaged by the Scots imprisoned in the cathedral after the Battle of Dunbar. The Neville Screen is a wonderful piece of work. Made in London by Henry Yevele from soft stone, sometimes called Caen stone or Dorsetshire clunch, it was brought, ready-carved and packed in chests, by sea to Newcastle. It was then moved on wagons to Durham, and seven masons were engaged for almost a year in erecting it. What are now empty niches on the screen were once adorned with 107 statues, probably removed when the monastery was dissolved by Henry VIII. Even without these, the Neville Screen is still a thing of great beauty.

The Neville family did not always, however, enjoy the most amicable of relationships with the cathedral. The Raby estate is today renowned for its two fine herds of deer, but in the 13th century Neville and Church actually came to blows over one of these creatures. One of the conditions on which the family held Raby was that each St Cuthbert's Day they had to present a deer to the abbey at Durham. For a long time this presentation was duly made, but in 1290, for some reason, Ralph, 3rd Lord Neville, decided that the time had come to turn the tables on the monks. He declared that he should be entertained by the prior and so should as many of his friends and servants as he chose to bring with him. The prior was astounded by the request and instructed that should a deer indeed be delivered it had to be refused. The abbey could not afford to feed so many people. On the appointed day Ralph Neville and his followers arrived at the north door of the cathedral carrying the stag, but instead of heading for the abbey kitchens they took the beast, to the accompaniment of blaring hunting horns and much rowdiness, to the Chapel of the Nine Altars. The monks duly refused to accept the offering but Neville simply ordered his men to take it to the kitchen and to cook it themselves. A fight broke out, the monks

18. Memorial to Bishop Shute Barrington, Durham Cathedral.

driving off the Raby men with some large and convenient candles. The argument was taken to litigation, the prior claiming that the routine of the church had been disrupted and Neville countering that he had suffered assault. Although both cases were subsequently allowed to lapse, the 3rd Lord Neville never again delivered a stag to the abbey.

A list of what was consumed in the abbey during the course of Whit Week, 1346 gives an insight into the diet enjoyed by the monks of Durham. This was to feed 70 monks and 16 novices as well as guests and helpers:

600 salt herrings, 400 white herrings, 30 salted salmon, 12 fresh salmon, 14 ling, 55 kelengs [?], 4 turbot, 2 horse-loads of white fish and a congr [conger eel], playc [plaice], sparling [?], and eels and fresh water fish, 9 carcases

19. A Billings engraving of 1841 showing the Great Clock in the south transept of the cathedral.

of oxen, salted, 1 carcase and a quarter, fresh, a quarter of an ox, fresh, 7 carcases and a half of swine in salt [pork], 6 carcases, fresh, 14 calves, 3 kids [young goats], and 26 sucking porkers, 5 stones of hog's lard, 4 stones of cheese, butter and milk, a pottle [half a gallon] of vinegar, a pottle of honey, 14 pounds of figs and raisins, 13 pounds of almonds, 8 pounds of rice, pepper, saffron, cinnamon and other spices and 1,300 eggs.

Just round the corner from the Neville tombs, past the Chantrey statue of Bishop Shute-Barrington (1791-1826), there is a clock in the south transept which has fascinated visitors for centuries. It was set up by Prior Castell, who administered the abbey between 1494 and 1519, and who made a carved oak case for it. The works and dials were renewed by Dean Hunt in 1632. How it survived the ravages of the Scottish prisoners is a mystery but it was probably useful to them in a purely practical way. It is also argued that a thistle carved over the upper dials caused it to be spared. The three dials over the main clockface record the month, the day and the phase of the moon. A doorway to the west of the clock gives access to the flight of 325 stairs which lead to the top of the great central tower. One of the most famous of the cathedral stories, connected with this tower, shows yet another link between the monks and the Nevilles of Raby; the tale concerns the Battle of Neville's Cross, an event feared by the monks at the outset and celebrated by them afterwards from their highest tower.

The incidents leading to the Battle of Neville's Cross are linked directly with the aftermath of the famous Battle of Crécy in 1346, the affray in which King Edward's son, the Black Prince, covered himself in so much glory. After this, the king moved to besiege Calais. The French king, who was an ally of the Scots, sent money and men to Scotland to help finance another invasion of England. Edward sent commissioners to King David II of Scotland offering to return Berwick to Scotland if he would leave England alone. Many in Scotland were anxious to accept this offer but David would have none of it. He knew full well that King Edward had taken England's best fighting men with him to France and that the country had rarely been so vulnerable, so he assembled a huge army and marched into England, inflicting damage and distress everywhere he went, burning Lanercost Priory, looting Hexham Abbey and exhibiting horrific barbarity to those he took prisoner. The Scottish army eventually came to the Beaurepaire (Bearpark/Redhills) area just outside Durham City, expecting an easy victory. Many of the English nobles and bishops who were not in France had, however, collected an army and were ready to defend the ancient city. Sykes describes it thus:

> On the 16th [October, 1346] the English forces lay in Auckland park, the next day they moved forward, and, after gaining the rising grounds, halted at Merrington, from whence the motions of the Scots on the western hills might be plainly distinguished. The English leaders hesitated whether to advance or to observe the enemy, and expect his attack in so favourable a position; the marshals and standard bearers moving a little forward, the troops insensibly followed them, and thus they proceeded slowly to Ferry-hill. Here a strong foraging party of the Scots, under Douglas, fell unexpectedly into the midst of the English troops, and were pursued with the loss of 500 men as far as Sunderland bridge. The English halted again on the high grounds above the Wear, but the standard bearers went forward, and the army moved slowly on in order of battle, leaving Durham on the right, to the moor near Neville's cross. Douglas, who had escaped from the slaughter of his pursuers, meanwhile reached the Scottish camp, and gave the first information of the approach of the English force. David had employed the preceding day in drawing out his troops (as if in defiance of opposition) on Durham moor, in order of battle, with standards flying, and had passed the night in Beaurepaire park and wood, without the precaution of a scout or sentinel on the watch. The prudent advice of Douglas to retreat to the hills and avoid an engagement was rejected with disdain, and the Scots advancing to meet the attack, the armies joined battle on the Red-hills, a piece of broken and irregular ground rising swiftly from the Wear. The Scots were formed in three divisions, under the king, the earl of Murray with Sir William Douglas and the high steward of Scotland. The English distributed their force in four

bodies; Lord Percy led the first, Lord Neville the second, Sir Thomas Rokeby, sheriff of Yorkshire, commanded the third, and a strong body of cavalry under Edward Baliol, formed the reserve. On a little hillock in the depth of Shawwood, called the Maiden's Bower, the prior with his attendants knelt around the holy corporax cloth of St. Cuthbert, which in obedience to a miraculous vision, was elevated on the point of a spear within sight of both armies. The city of Durham lay in dreadful suspense, a prize to the conqueror; and whilst the remaining brethren of the convent, poured forth their hymns and prayers from the highest towers of the cathedral, their eyes wandered with anxious doubt over the field of approaching combat. The Scots were severely galled as they advanced by the English archers; and John Graham, impatient at seeing his men fall without the means of resistance, requested of the king an hundred lancers to break the archers; his request was denied and the troops were ordered to keep the line of battle. Actuated at once by courage and indignation, Graham threw himself singly or with few attendants amongst the archers, dispersed them on every side, and fought till his horse was struck by a broad arrow, and himself wounded and bleeding, was scarcely able to regain the ranks of his countrymen with life. The high steward immediately led his division to the charge with broad swords and battle axes; the archers were driven back through Lord Percy's division, which they disordered in their retreat; and the Scots pursuing their advantage, threw the whole of the body into confusion. Victory hovered on the side of the invaders, but the day was restored by the courage and decision of Edward Baliol. With a powerful body of cavalry, he made an impetuous charge on the high steward's divisions and drove them from the field. King David was meanwhile engaged with equal fortunes against Lord Neville; and Baliol suffering the high steward to retreat unmolested threw himself on the flank of the royal troops which was left uncovered by his flight. The disorder of the Scots became irretrievable, and their third body, under the earl of Murray, were cut to pieces amongst the inclosures which prevented their escape. After all was lost, a gallant band of nobles formed themselves around their king, and fought with the courage of despair, till only eight of their number survived. David, after receiving two arrow wounds, and resisting several attempts to take him captive, was compelled to surrender to John Copeland, a Northumbrian esquire, two of whose teeth he dashed out with his clenched steel gauntlet. Besides the king, the earls of Fife and Monteith, and Sir William Douglas, were made prisoners; the earls of Murray and Strathmore, John and Alan Steward, and a long list of Scottish nobility, were amongst the slain. Of the English leaders, Lord Hastings alone fell. Copeland was rewarded by the English king with £500 a year in land, and made a knight banneret. Out of an army of 30,000 Scots and French auxiliaries, 15,000 were left dead upon the field, whilst the loss of the English was very trifling.

According to some early sources, the monks watching the battle from the central tower began to sing with joy when they knew that the Scots had been routed. On the anniversary of the battle each year for a considerable time thereafter a party of monks made its way to the top of the tower and sang three anthems, one to each point of the compass except to the west, where the battle had been fought. The ceremony continues to this day, although it now takes place on Ascension Day. Choristers explain that after a climb of 325 steps they have breath enough left to allow them not only to sing but to sing slightly more quickly than normal, this being ascribed to a quickening of the pulse, either because of excitement or exertion. How continuous this tradition of tower-singing has been is debatable; its date has been

20. Central tower of Durham Cathedral.

21. The bishop's throne in the cathedral, from *The Graphic*, 1883.

22. A Billings engraving of 1841 showing the bishop's throne in the cathedral.

changed on several occa-
sions, notably when it was
moved to Oak Apple Day,
29 May, in honour of the
return of King Charles II.

A walk along the south
aisle of the choir, past the
Durham Light Infantry
chapel, leads to the eastern-
most end of the cathedral,
the Chapel of the Nine
Altars with its magnificent
rose, or wheel, window,
the present one dating
from the late 19th century.
It was originally glazed
between 1409 and 1413 by
Richard Pickeringe but
was badly damaged at the
end of the 18th century by
George Nicholson, of
whose restoration more
follows. The chapel is
divided into three bays of
unequal size. Before the
Reformation there were
nine altars against the east
wall. From north to south
their dedications were to
St Michael the Archangel,
St Aidan and St Helen,
St Peter and St Paul,
St Martin, St Cuthbert and
St Bede, St Oswald and
St Laurence, St Thomas of

23.   Modern carving in wood of St Cuthbert in the cloisters of the
cathedral.

Canterbury and St Katherine, St John the Baptist and St Margaret, the last to
St Andrew and St Mary Magdalene. The altars were separated by wooden partitions
into which were built cupboards to hold vestments. There was also a wooden canopy
over each altar. At the north end of the chapel is a charming memorial to Bishop
William Van Mildert, founder of Durham University and technically the last of the
prince bishops of Durham. Buried just in front of his statue lies the 14th-century
Bishop Antony Bek, the first person since Cuthbert to be allowed burial in the
cathedral. Just west of Bek's grave is the memorial to the Victorian bishop, Joseph
Barber Lightfoot, reputed to have been the finest and most able English theologian
of his time. Bishop Walter Skirlaw (1388-1405) is buried nearby. A few steps here lead

into the choir, in which there is the tomb of Bishop Thomas Hatfield (1345-81), founder of Durham College, now Trinity College, Oxford. This, however, is no simple tomb for it is incorporated within the episcopal throne, 'the highest bishop's throne in Christendom'.

Durham Cathedral today is far more than a memorial to the past or some relic of a bygone age. It is a tribute to all who have served in it over the centuries, and also much more. This is a living, working church, a house of God which has long been a focus for Cuthbert's people, the people of the City and County of Durham. Time, admittedly, may be seen to stand still when the strains of the great organ swell and reach into the cathedral's most secret corners, when the choir is in full voice, or in quiet moments when the visitors have gone, but there are new features too. In the ancient cloisters, for example, there stands Fenwick Lawson's massive wooden carving of St Cuthbert, which dates from 1981, a statue derided by many. It did not fit, they said; it was ugly, they claimed; it was an insult to the saint's memory. The piece was carved from a huge elm tree which had been blighted by Dutch Elm disease, and used to stand between the north door of the cathedral and the old grammar school. Now the wood has mellowed and cracked with the passing seasons, and rain and wind, frost and snow have played their part in making the piece a feature, almost part of the fabric, of the cathedral. Also new is some of the stained glass, notably the Marks and Spencer window, more properly known as the Daily Bread window, created by Mark Angus and placed to the west of the great north door. The window was dedicated in 1984. It pictures the Last Supper in brilliant colours and modern design and was given by the Durham branch of Marks and Spencer to commemorate the firm's centenary. There are those who do not like this window, but there were doubtless many in the past who failed to be inspired by much of what is now in the cathedral when it was new. Tradition has a hallowed place but tradition is a platform on which progress builds.

There have been times at Durham, however, when supposed progress, 'a little learning', was a very dangerous concept; dangerous, that is, for posterity. The cathedral at Durham was seriously threatened and much damaged in the late 18th century by men who felt that they were doing the right thing. It all started late in the 1770s when a local architect, John Wooler, began to look at the cathedral and informed the Dean and Chapter that it was in an alarmingly dangerous condition. Virtually every part of the building, he suggested, was in need of urgent repair. His assistant, George Nicholson, having just finished his work on Prebends' Bridge, began to 'restore' the fabric, chiselling deep into the exterior walls and removing windows, particularly the rose window in the east end. Nicholson's work was taken up by James Wyatt, known to local historians today as 'The Destroyer'. Workmen continued to chisel away the outside stonework, often cutting as deep as four inches. Wyatt demolished practically all of the beautiful Norman chapter house, and planned to pull down the Galilee chapel to make way for a carriage drive up to the great west door, which he proposed to reopen. Before this project was actually terminated, Wyatt had already removed the lead from the roof. He had also wanted to erect a spire on the central tower and to raise the floor level of the Chapel of the Nine Altars to that of the rest of the cathedral. Neither proposal was allowed to proceed. In the 1840s there were yet more attempts to alter the cathedral but the changes made were not as devastating as those undertaken or intended by Nicholson and Wyatt.

No visitor should leave Durham Cathedral without visiting the treasury and seeing St Cuthbert's own possessions, his altar, his comb and his pectoral cross. Also on view are gifts made at his shrine over the years and substantial fragments of his oak coffin, many still displaying the original seventh-century carving. Through these items St Cuthbert somehow seems to reach across the centuries. No matter what its official dedication, Durham Cathedral has always been and always will be Cuthbert's church.

Chapter Four

Durham Castle and Palace Green

Durham City has twin architectural and historical jewels, its magnificent cathedral and its ancient and imposing castle, which both survive today as testaments to the traumas of 1,000 years.

Although the basis of the present castle buildings was begun in 1072 by Waltheof, Earl of Northumberland, at the order of William the Conqueror himself, there were undoubtedly earlier defensive works on and near the present lofty, naturally-defended site. These were used by the Saxon defenders against the unsuccessful siege by the Scottish King Malcolm in 1006 and again some 30 years later when the Scots, this time led by King Duncan, were equally frustrated. Unlike the cathedral Durham Castle does not rest on secure rock foundations, and has required a great deal of restoration over the centuries to preserve what is seen today. Bishop Hugh Pudsey's 12th-century hall, for example, was in imminent danger of collapsing just a short time after it was completed; further consolidation was required six centuries later. The stone of which the castle is built is not especially hard; as a result the building has had to be refaced on several occasions. One of these 'restorations' was under-taken in the 18th century by the infamous James Wyatt. The foundations have several times seemed to be in danger of collapse and in the 1930s an appeal had to be launched to save the building. Although today it is the term-time home of students at Durham's University College, the castle was, until 1837, inhabited or superintended by the prince bishops of Durham, a tenure relinquished only on the death of William van Mildert in 1836.

As the Normans took over England after their victory in 1066 at the Battle of Hastings, they erected a multitude of motte and bailey castles, basically wooden strong-houses, on an artificial mound where no other convenient high ground existed, surrounded by a strong wooden fence and moat, or ditch, beyond which was another fenced enclosure or bailey. This was the area where animals and people from the area nearby could find protection when there was danger of attack, where horses could be stabled and supplies stored. As time passed, many of the strong-houses became stone castles, their wooden palisades being replaced by more substantial stone walls. Durham had both an inner and outer bailey, and substantial parts of the old bailey walls can still be seen in many of the present Bailey gardens, particularly in nos. 3 and 4 North Bailey. The outer bailey, especially, is now rather difficult to discern. Little now remains, however, of the original Norman castle. The stone of that building has obviously been re-used elsewhere on the site but the only original work is the chapel and the undercroft. Of the large hall built on the north side of the courtyard by Bishop Pudsey a century later, there is more substantial evidence but it, too, has been much altered. A century later Bishop Bek began construction of what is now the Great Hall on the western side of the courtyard, a huge room added to by

24. Durham Castle and Palace Green.

Bishop Hatfield in the middle of the 14th century. It was Hatfield, too, who undertook one of the rebuildings of the keep.

Durham Castle has not always been purely a fortress, a bastion against Scottish incursions. Today's visitor will notice that, despite its huge proportions, the building has a real welcoming warmth, a feature which is not accidental. In the early years of the 16th century the bishops and their retainers seem to have decided that, as there was no longer need for the building to serve as a major fortress, it could be converted into a comfortable lodging. It was then that the shell of the present kitchens was added along with a new chapel. By the time the Civil War had drawn to a close in the mid-17th century, the castle was gradually taking on a new role. Starting with John Cosin, subsequent bishops used the building for hospitality and to demonstrate their great wealth and power.

If it is true that walls have ears, it would be interesting to hear what stories would unfold if the walls of Durham Castle could talk, for the building has welcomed a wealth of visitors in its time. Many English monarchs have been entertained here including Edward III, Charles I, James II and all of the monarchs of the House of Windsor including Queen Elizabeth II, as well as a number of Scottish rulers. Accommodation was also provided until 1971 for Her Majesty's Assize Judges. Hospitality has always been on a lavish scale. For example, when Bishop Cosin was preparing for the arrival of the assize judges in August 1661, the provisions purchased to entertain them included:

> a fat oxe, 9 pigeons, 24 ducks, 16 geese, 36 turkeys, a cage of sturgeon from Darlington, mutton, veal and other butcher meat, ham, neats' tongues, a Holland cheese, sweetmeats wet and dry, oranges and lemons, three loads of malt brewed in the house, three dozen bottles of canary wine, two dozen bottles of sack and a tun of French wine.

The total cost was £140. More than 150 years later, on 3 October 1827 Bishop Van Mildert hosted a banquet in the Great Hall in honour of the Duke of Wellington. About fifty other men were present as guests, including Sir Walter Scott. Today, when the students are not in residence, the castle continues its tradition of hospitality by providing excellent conference facilities.

The courtyard of the castle is an irregular shape and is entered via a Norman-cored gateway; much of the rest of this entrance was constructed by James Wyatt. The massive studded gates are early 17th-century. The keep itself, as seen today, is largely the work of the architect Anthony Salvin who, in 1840, rebuilt the ruins of the 14th-century construction. The Great Hall, created by Bek, extended by Hatfield 50 years later and subsequently reduced to its original size by Bishop Fox, who also created the adjoining kitchens, is a magnificent feature. Over 100 ft. long and 45 ft. high, its walls are decorated with arms and banners, along with portraits of the great and famous associated with Durham; included is a painting of Durham University's first student, John Cundill. The large stained-glass window by Kempe at the north end dates from 1882, when it was created to celebrate Durham University's 50th birthday. At the opposite end of the hall is the modern 'minstrels' gallery'.

The Black Staircase, dating from the mid-1660s, stands between the Great Hall and Bishop Pudsey's building, and is sometimes known as Bishop Cosin's staircase. Displaying a quite amazing camber, it is 57 ft. high, climbs four storeys and, except for its beautifully-carved willow panels, is made completely of oak. It is a staircase to be not simply used but savoured. The small Norman chapel, dating from c.1080, was probably unused from the inauguration of Bishop Tunstall's chapel in 1542 until its reintroduction as a place of worship in 1952. Tunstall's creation was subsequently enlarged by Bishops Cosin and Crewe; especially noteworthy in this chapel are its fine proportions and its beautiful woodwork, some brought from the cathedral, some from Auckland Palace and some inserted since the foundation of the university.

25. Interior of the Hall, University College, from *The Graphic*, 1883.

26. The staircase in the castle, from *The Graphic*, 1883.

27. John Cosin, Bishop of Durham, 1660-72.

One of the most amusing men ever to occupy a student's room in the keep of Durham Castle was Edward, later the Rev. Edward, Bradley, better known to posterity as the author and cartoonist Cuthbert Bede. Born the son of a doctor in March 1827, he was educated first at Kidderminster Grammar School and, in 1845, admitted as a theology undergraduate of the fairly new University of Durham. On graduating in 1848, Bradley spent some time in Oxford before his ordination in 1850, after which he took up the post of Rector of Stretton, in Rutland. Using the pseudonym of 'Cuthbert Bede', borrowed from the two great saints buried in the Cathedral, Bradley penned some amusing accounts of university life as it was in his day. It was while still an undergraduate that he drew a series of sketches which he titled 'Ye Freshmonne, his adventures at University College, Durham'. It is interesting to note that in Bradley's day, 'Ye Freshmonne', presumably like all undergraduates and other travellers to Durham, arrived at Gilesgate railway station – not the one in use today. Spending his first night at one of the *The Waterloo* inns, and there were two of the same name adjacent to each other in Old Elvet, he dreams that he has become a bishop, but is rudely awakened to spend the next day in pursuit of suitable lodgings which he eventually finds in 'Ye Castle'. When Bradley later tried to sell a number of his sketches to *Punch* magazine, he was told that he must adapt them to represent Oxford University. Durham was unacceptable as a backdrop.

Bradley was also one of the first people to think of producing a Christmas card. It is now widely accepted that the designer of the first Christmas card was John Horsley, who was commissioned to produce it in 1843 by the director of London's Victoria and Albert Museum, Henry Cole. Edward Bradley conceived the idea of a Christmas card during his first term at Durham in 1845; his card, when produced by Mark Lambert of Newcastle, measured 3¾ by 2½ ins. and carried the greeting 'Wyshinge you the compliments of the season'. Showing holly, ivy and mistletoe, the card was printed in four colours. Bradley wrote 22 books as well as being a regular contributor to *Punch*, *The Illustrated London News* and *The Field*. At the time of his death, in 1889, he was Vicar of Grantham.

As an undergraduate in the castle, Bradley would have known Palace Green and its buildings very well. The large and carefully tended expanse of lawn between castle and cathedral is enclosed on its east and west sides by two beautiful ranges of buildings. This great space was created at the beginning of the 12th century, when Bishop Flambard demolished the clutter of houses and Market Place which occupied the area between the two then-unfinished Norman buildings. The people who had lived there probably moved across to the river to Crossgate and Framwellgate.

The first building on the left as the Green proper is entered from Owengate was adapted by Anthony Salvin in 1841 from the bishop's coach-house and stables, and is now used as two garages and a public lavatory. Set back from it is a new university accommodation block, totally in keeping with the character and style of the area. Just to the south of it is a rare and beautifully preserved example of an acorn-capped Victorian pillar box. The next building on this east side is the brick-built Bishop Cosin's Hall, a late 17th-century three-storey house with a wonderful elaborate hood to its main entrance. Formerly known as Archdeacon's Inn, it was used as a hall of residence by the university until 1864.

The arms of Bishop John Cosin are still to be seen over the main doorway of the stone-built almshouses, founded in 1666 and replacing Bishop Langley's dilapidated song and grammar schools of 1414. The almshouses accommodated eight poor people, four men and four women, while the north and south ends of the building were used as schools, one for grammar, the other for plainsong and the art of writing. Next along is the Pemberton Building, looking much older but actually dating only from 1931. On the corner of this range and Dun Cow Lane, once

28. Victorian pillar box, Palace Green.

29 a & b. Edward Bradley's *Ye Freshmonne* cartoons, parts one and two (courtesy of Durham Union Society).

YE FRESHMONNE HIS ADVENTURES AT UNIV. COLL. DURHAM. Part II.

BEING MATRICULATED HE ASSUMETH THE CAP & GOWN & UNDER THE DELUSION THAT THEY BECOME

HIM, HE DISPORTETH HIMSELF ON THE BANKS TO THE GREAT AMUSEMENT OF MANY YOUNG LADIES

AND ALARM OF SEVERAL BABIES, WHO WITH THEIR NURSES ARE ALWAYS TO BE MET THERE

HE CAPPETH YE DEAN AND THEN GOETH INTO HALL TO DINNER

WHEN, BEING ASKED WHAT HE WILL TAKE HE NAMETH "CHICKEN" BUT IS TOLD THAT THE

FARE IS NOT FOWL HE IS INVITED TO THE "FRESHMAN'S WINE" OF WHICH HE DRAWS A MENTAL PICTURE

BUT FINDS THE REALITY FAR BEYOND HIS EXPECTATION AFTER HAVING HIS HEALTH DRUNK AS A JOLLY GOOD FELLOW, HE TRIS TO

SHEW HE IS ONE BY TAKING TOO MUCH WINE UNDER THE INFLUENCE OF WHICH HE IS ASSISTED TO HIS OWN ROOMS

HE PASSES AN UNEASY NIGHT ON HIS HEARTH-RUG, AND IS FOUND THERE BY THE BED-MAKER IN THE MORNING

30. Bishop Cosin's almshouses of 1666, Palace Green.

31. Entrance to Bishop Cosin's almshouses, Palace Green.

32. The Tudor-style Pemberton building, built in 1931, Palace Green.

33. On the left, the old Grammar School of 1661 and, on the right, the former diocesan registry of 1822, both on Palace Green.

known as Lykegate or Lydgate, the place where coffins were rested, stands Abbey House, built to three storeys early in the 18th century although parts of it are earlier.

The buildings to the west of Palace Green begin at the south end with the old grammar school, serving that purpose from 1661 to 1844 and now used by the university. Adjoining it is Divinity House, formerly occupied by the school's headmaster and, on occasion, by some of the pupils. On a rise in the ground between the old grammar school and the cathedral is a tall and tapering stone cross, reminiscent in style of the early Saxon crosses. Standing on a plinth, it was erected in 1905 to the memory of 'The Officers, N.C.O.s and Men of the Durham Light Infantry who were killed in action or died of wounds or disease in the South African Campaign, 1899 to 1902'. Separating the old school from the other buildings on this side of the Green is Windy Gap, a steep vennel (narrow alley) giving access to the riverbank.

At the other side of Windy Gap are buildings associated with the university library. First, erected in 1822 on the site of the old assize courts of Bishop Cosin, is what was the Diocesan Registry and is now part of the library. A plaque records that a county courthouse stood on this site from 1588 to 1811. The present building was passed to the Union Society in 1935 and then to the library in 1978. Beside it is Anthony Salvin's university library of 1858 with George Pace's 1968 extension, best viewed

34. University library, Palace Green.

35. Civic pride on Palace Green – the presentation, in 1880, of a silver bugle by the ladies of Durham to the Durham Volunteer Rifle Corps.

from the riverbank. Next door is Bishop Cosin's library, built by John Longstaffe at the bishop's expense in 1669, primarily for the use of the clergy of his diocese. Cosin's arms are over the main door. An additional entrance was added in about 1833 as an access to the collection for students of the new university. A story still told, although it cannot be substantiated, is that one Thomas Blakiston, employed by Cosin to catalogue his books, reached the letter 'D' and then ran away with the bishop's daughter!

Finally in this western range of buildings is the Exchequer and Chancery, which used to house the Mint, for some of the bishops coined their own money, and Palatinate Court, erected by Bishop Neville in about 1450. Its ground floor is now below the level of the street. Situated on the cobbles at the north-east corner of the Green, just in front of the wall behind which is the Master's House, there is a small, round, stone plinth. Affixed to it is a plaque which records the true importance of the area of Palace Green. It reads: '1987. In accord with the principles of the World Heritage Convention, Durham Cathedral and Castle have been designated a World Heritage Site, one of a number of protected areas of outstanding natural and cultural significance in our common heritage. UNESCO'.

Chapter Five

The University of Durham

For centuries there were just two universities in England, those at Oxford and Cambridge, enjoying and exploiting their duopoly. Famous as they were, however, they were inadequate, not simply because they were small but because, for undergraduates and their parents, they were expensive institutions, prohibitively costly for all but the comparatively wealthy. Nor did the two universities always serve their students well, particularly in respect of the tutorial system which was regarded as being, at the start of the 19th century, rather less than useful. The admission system was inadequate too. Oxford refused to admit any students who were dissenters while Cambridge admitted them but would not award them degrees. There was, therefore, in the 1820s general dissatisfaction throughout the land about the state of the English university system. As well as this, there was a strengthening movement which advocated better education at all levels for 'the masses', although there were still many who steadfastly opposed such revolutionary ideas.

All sorts of plans and ideas were in the air but the catalyst in the university debate was probably an open letter in *The Times* in 1825 from the poet Thomas Campbell, in which he suggested a university in London. Just three years later, after frenzied activity by many people, 557 students were enrolled in the new foundation. Other cities, including Liverpool, Newcastle-upon-Tyne and York, were also working towards the foundation of their own universities; learned men debated the issues and sought funds to implement their ideas, but it was to be the little City of Durham which would lead the field – and in more ways than one.

This 19th-century attempt to establish a university at Durham was not the first. For many years, since the end of the 13th century, the Bishops of Durham had sent able young men to Durham Hall, later renamed Trinity College, at Oxford. When Henry VIII had ordered the dissolution of the monastery at Durham, there were efforts made to channel some of the former monastic revenues into the establishment of a college in the city, but the attempt came to nothing. All Durham's links with Trinity College were severed in 1556.

In 1657, Parliament having been petitioned on the matter three times by people in Durham County, Oliver Cromwell approached the Speaker of the House of Commons advocating the conversion of several old chapter houses at Durham Cathedral at Durham into a college. Cromwell argued for the scheme on the grounds that it would do much to promote 'learning and piety in these poore, rude and ignorant parts'. The scheme called for an establishment comprising a provost, two senior fellows, four professors, four tutors and four schoolmasters for 24 scholars and 12 exhibitioners. Perceiving the potential threat, however, the vice-chancellor of Oxford University sent embassies to London to object most strongly to this plan. He need not have worried unduly because the death of Oliver Cromwell in 1658, the end of the Commonwealth and restoration of King Charles II to the English throne in 1660 ended the venture.

The next attempt was not merely the result of concern over the state of education in England but also, in many ways, because of ill-feeling about poor representation of the people across the land, and about the power and wealth enjoyed by the clergy and the Durham clergy in particular. Earl Grey's government had been elected after having promised wide-ranging reforms. The new king, William IV, was ready to back parliamentary reform so, in 1831, Grey and his cabinet brought in their famous Reform Bill. After several attempts, riots across the country and a state of near-revolution, the bill was passed and became law. Grey had demonstrated his determination not to be brow-beaten by the likes of the Duke of Wellington, and he had broken the monopoly of power once enjoyed by the aristocratic landowners. This was merely the beginning of Grey's reforms.

In the late 18th and early 19th century many of the Durham clergy were very wealthy in comparison with their counterparts elsewhere. This was largely because of the revenue derived from the coal deposits beneath the Church's land. Some Durham clergymen held other livings as well as those in the county, a system known as 'plurality', thus gaining even greater incomes. Along with the outcry for parliamentary reform came a call for the overhaul of what was perceived to be an iniquitous system. Also to come under close scrutiny was the income, or reported income, of the Bishop of Durham. Some of the Durham clergy were aware of the storm about to break over them, and decided that they were best-advised to do nothing and await the thunder, while others felt that action needed to be taken immediately to retain at least some of the Church funds within the county and to appropriate them for good purpose. One of those who had this latter vision was Bishop van Mildert, an opponent of parliamentary reform, who had ascended the episcopal throne in 1826 as successor to Shute Barrington. It was in July 1831 that Bishop van Mildert and others conceived the idea of diverting Church funds into the creation of a University of Durham. It was later to be claimed that there were few clerical supporters of the new scheme, but at the time it received enthusiastic support from a lot of people. The bishop was asked by some to lower his academic sights but argued that nothing less than 'a university with the power of granting degrees would answer the expectations of the public'.

On 4 July 1832, the Royal Assent was given to the Bill for the establishment of a university at Durham, 'An act to enable the dean and chapter of Durham to appropriate part of the property of their church to the establishment of a university in connexion therewith for the advancement of learning'. Like Oxford and Cambridge, however, the new university would award degrees only to those students who recognised the supreme authority of the king and adhered to the Book of Common Prayer; in other words, dissenters could attend lectures but could progress no further. The new university was, after all, administered and controlled by the dean and chapter of Durham and had been established in connection with the Cathedral Church of Durham. These bodies did not intend to undermine their own foundations. Conversely, it was never the intention of the founders of Durham University that it should be no more than a northern training ground for Anglican priests. The

36.   Examination of the students of the University of Durham, 1842.

doctrines of the Church of England were to be observed by the students but subjects other than divinity were to be studied, including, as one cleric put it, 'the numerous tribes of medical sciences with names terminating in -ogy'. On the other hand, though, it was not until 1908 that compulsory student attendance at church on Sundays was abolished; only in 1910 did the dean and chapter finally relinquish control over the university.

The Church was left to foot most of the bills for the setting up of the new university, financial help from the laity not being as forthcoming as had been expected. Bishop van Mildert donated Durham Castle and several thousand pounds as his contribution, but on his death in 1836 funds were still less than needed. The old castle was itself a great drain on the university coffers. Various measures were taken to improve and consolidate the funding of the new establishment, but by 1857 serious thought was being given to closing down the entire enterprise. Finance was reorganised, however, new funds were found and the venture continued, although it was claimed that students at Durham had to meet expenses as heavy as those encountered by their counterparts at Oxford and Cambridge.

In 1834 Newcastle-upon-Tyne, having earlier failed to secure its own university, was pacified by having the Newcastle-upon-Tyne College for Medicine in connection with the University of Durham sited there. It was not until 1870 that this college became a complete part of Durham University. Most radical of all the developments associated with the creation of Durham University was the foundation there in 1837 of a School of Civil Engineering, probably the first in the land. It eventually failed because funds could not be found either to award scholarships to engineering students, or to establish a chair in the subject.

Durham University is an institution in which most students are resident in one of the constituent colleges while receiving their education in various parts of the university. The colleges and university buildings are scattered throughout the city, some in its very heart, others in the more leafy suburbs, some easily recognisable, others more discreet. University College, based in and around Durham Castle, is the oldest of the Durham colleges, having been established with the university in 1832. Women were not admitted to University College until 1987. Hatfield College, in North Bailey and just a short distance from Palace Green, was founded in 1846 and named after the 14th-century Bishop Thomas Hatfield. The intention was to provide a residence for young men who did not have the financial resources to live in University College, and the initial housing was in the elegant 18th-century *Red Lion* coaching inn. With its lower fees, Hatfield College provided a useful resource for the university, as a result of which the Archdeacon's Inn was reopened in 1851 and renamed Bishop Cosin's Hall. It remained open for just 13 years.

Although the combined college of St Bede and St Hild became a full member of the university only in 1979, ceasing at that time to be a College of Education, the two separate establishments have a long and distinguished history. The College of the Venerable Bede was founded at Durham in 1839 as a Church of England college to train young men as schoolteachers. It thus predates Hatfield College as a foundation. Its first buildings were established between 1845 and 1847, with further extensions between then and 1858, and more in 1875. One of Durham's modern architectural gems is the beautiful college chapel designed by Seely and Paget, built on the eve of the outbreak of World War II, and described, (by Pevsner) as an 'outstanding work of modern ecclesiastical architecture'. St Hild's College, for intending women teachers, dates from 1858. The west wing was added in 1907, the chapel in 1912 and the east wing in 1925. Both colleges had more modern buildings added in the middle of the 20th century. Bede accepted degree students for the first time in 1892 while Hild's ladies were admitted for degree in 1896, a year after the university started to grant degrees to women.

As the university grew, it accepted that not all students needed to be members of a college. Such 'unattached' students were admitted from 1871 and some formed themselves into societies. One such was St Cuthbert's Society, formed in 1888, followed in 1899 by a hostel for women students, Abbey House on the peninsula. In 1919 this became St Mary's College, housed since 1952 in a virtual French château on Elvet Hill. A new building was added in 1962. St Aidan's College, on Windmill Hill since 1964, was another establishment which started life as a non-collegiate group for women students; the main building was designed by Sir Basil Spence. Nestling beneath the great east end of the cathedral, St Chad's College, established in 1904, is situated in the North Bailey. A little way along the road, in the South Bailey, is St John's College, set up in 1909. Both foundations were originally for theological students and both can boast 18th-century building as part of their premises.

37. Ushaw College, near Durham.

38. Ushaw College, the chapel.

Many of the Durham colleges are post-World War II and have been established to the south of the city. The first of these was Grey College, built on Fountains Field, whose first students were admitted in 1959. It was named after the great parliamentary reformer, the second Earl Grey. Taking its name from one of the university's founders is Van Mildert College which admitted its first students in 1965 while nearby Trevelyan College opened its doors in 1967. Named after the famous historian G. M. Trevelyan, a former chancellor of the university, in 1969 it won a Civic Trust Award. Collingwood College, the first in Durham to be conceived and constructed as a fully co-educational residential college, dates from 1972 and is named after the distinguished Cambridge mathematician Sir Edward Collingwood, a former Chairman of the Council of the University of Durham. The architects were Richard Sheppard, Robson and Partners. Facilities for graduate students are catered for in various parts of the university but especially by the Graduate Society, founded in 1965. Four miles to the west of Durham City, near the village of Bearpark, is Ushaw College, a Roman Catholic seminary opened on its present site in 1808. In 1968, Ushaw College was licensed as a hall of residence for Durham University.

Durham University today is a collegiate institution, boasting one of the most extensive and comprehensive ranges of teaching and research facilities available anywhere in Britain. Nor is this university one which rests on its past successes, for new developments are always in evidence, as they have been from its inception, keeping pace with new thinking and new technologies while still retaining old and trusted values.

Chapter Six

The Market Place

Although the most famous parts of Durham are the cathedral and the castle, the undoubted centre of the city is the ancient Market Place, now virtually a pedestrian precinct. The policeman in his box may no longer direct the traffic using his bank of television monitors but any driver who attempts to negotiate the Market Place still finds himself faced with a daunting task.

Durham Market Place, created by Bishop Flambard early in the 12th century, is not large but it is very attractive. The ancient routes into it from Elvet Bridge via Fleshergate and Framwellgate Bridge via Silver Street are much as they have been for centuries. The route from Claypath and Gilesgate is, however, undercut by a new road which uses two new bridges across the Wear. Slip roads from the new carriageway now feed into the old road.

39. Durham, from the lower end of Framwell Gate.

The focal point of the Market Place is an equestrian statue of Charles William Vane Stewart, 3rd Marquess of Londonderry, 1st Earl Vane and Baron Stewart of Stewarts Court (1778-1854) in the uniform of a hussar. He was ancestrally connected with the monarchs of Scotland. Initially a soldier and politician, the Marquess became Lord Lieutenant of Durham and is remembered today as the founder of Seaham Harbour on the Durham coast. The statue, made of plaster coated with copper, an early example of electroplating, was executed by a sculptor from Milan, Raffaelle Monti. The story is told that so proud was Monti of his statue that he offered a reward to anyone who could find fault with it. Many tried; they wondered if the uniform might be incorrect in some small detail; the muscle structure of the horse might not be all it should be; the saddle might not be an accurate representation. Many attempted to find fault but all failed until there came to Durham one day an old, blind beggar. He asked that he should be allowed to try for the prize. Derision greeted his challenge but he was at last hoisted up to the platform to try his luck. Only a few minutes later he asked to be lowered again to the ground. The crowd which had gathered laughed at his ungainly descent and began to disperse, but then the blind beggar announced that he had found a fault. A stunned silence was followed by an uproar of laughter. Gradually, the crowd fell silent. What, they asked him, was the mistake made by one of the greatest sculptors in the world? The beggar pointed towards his mouth and told the assembly that the horse had no tongue.

When they realised just how large the statue was to be, the City Council tried to have it erected on Palace Green instead of in the Market Place. They failed in their endeavour and at the statue's unveiling on 2 December 1861 there were present units of the North Durham Militia, Durham City Rifle Volunteers, Sunderland Rifle Volunteers and Seaham Artillery Volunteers. The statue was restored in 1952. The Londonderry statue occupies the site of the old market house but for it to be in Durham Market Place at all is, in a way, unusual, considering the relationship the 3rd Marquess had with some of the men of Durham who, in later years, so often marched past the 'Bold Sabreur', as he was known.

Despite having been a brilliant and daring soldier, friend of the great and famous of his day and doer of good deeds, the 3rd Marquess of Londonderry was not popular with Durham's miners, many of them his employees. In 1822 Stewart inherited his title, as well as the lucrative family estates in Ireland, when his half-brother the 2nd Marquess of Londonderry, Robert Stewart, Viscount Castlereagh, Foreign Secretary and Leader of the House of Commons, committed suicide. Three years earlier, he had married Frances Anne Vane-Tempest, an heiress to estates in Ireland and County Durham. At the same time he changed his name to Vane. Born in Dublin in 1778, he was educated at Eton College. When just 16, Charles acquired a commission in the army in MacNamara's Regiment. Just a year later he had risen to the rank of major in the 106th Foot from which he moved, after distinguished service in the Netherlands and Germany, to the Royal Irish Dragoons. Acquiring great fame as a cavalry commander, Stewart served under Sir John Moore and the Duke of Wellington. By 1808 he led the Hussar Brigade, subsequently served as Adjutant-General to Wellington and took over from the Prince Regent as Colonel of the 10th Hussars and then the 2nd Life Guards. As a statesman, he served as British

Ambassador to Vienna. After his marriage, Charles Stewart went to live a few miles north of Stockton at Wynyard Park and bought another estate, including several collieries, at Seaham. As well as sinking new, deep, coastal mineshafts, he constructed a railway to carry his coal to Sunderland. The harbour and docks he created as Seaham Harbour had taken three years to complete when they were opened in 1831.

What alienated the 3rd Marquess from the common people of Durham was his entrenched opposition to reform of almost any sort. He would not allow his mines to be inspected, he opposed the raising of the statutory school leaving age to twelve, was not in favour of the 1832 Reform Bill, did all he could to prevent the formation of mining trade unions, and brought Cornish tin miners to the county to break a strike of his own colliery employees. It must be said in his defence that Londonderry was a man of his time and a product of the system which raised him, feeling that everything and everyone had a rightful place. He fought two duels during his life

40.   Statue of third Marquess of Londonderry, the Market Place.

and was once set upon by a Durham mob. Miners have long memories, however, and it is interesting to note that although one of the 3rd Marquess's descendants supported Prime Minister Ramsay MacDonald in his last parliamentary election, the premier was defeated by miners' champion Emmanuel 'Manny' Shinwell.

The Marquess's wife, Lady Frances Anne, had a very different relationship with the miners. On several recorded occasions she entertained 'upwards of 3,000 pitmen and workpeople employed on her ladyship's collieries' to festivities which included the serving of 'eight bullocks, fifteen sheep, a ton of plum pudding, a ton and a half of bread, one hundred bushels of potatoes and fifty barrels of ale'. She was also the first person to suggest the setting up of funds to provide aged miners with retirement homes, an idea which came to fruition some 40 years afterwards.

Just to the south of the statue of Lord Londonderry and his horse is another statue which was absent from the Market Place for a long time. This is of Neptune and it was restored to its present Market Place site in May 1991. The statue was originally given to the city in 1729 by George Bowes, M.P. of Gibside and Streatlam, as a symbol of the scheme to link Durham City to the sea by improved navigation of the River Wear. There were four such schemes proposed, none of which came to fruition. At first the statue stood on top of the Market Place wellheads, very close to its present site, finding a new home in 1863 on top of E. R. Robson's replacement well-head fountain. The old man of the sea also topped the new pant (fountain) of 1902. In 1923 the statue was moved to Durham's Wharton Park whence it was removed, having been struck by lightning, for restoration in 1986 by Andrew Naylor of Telford.

One of Durham's best-known historians, Thomas Hutchinson, wrote in 1787 that in the Market Place

> is a fluent fountain of excellent water, which supplies the greatest part of the town. The reservoir is built up in an elegant form, and ornamented with a fine statue of Neptune. In the year 1450, Tho. Billington, esq; granted to the city for ever, a spring of water in his manor of Sidgate with liberty to convey the same by pipes, etc. to a reservoir in the Market Place for the public use, at thirteen-pence a year rent.

Repairs to and maintenance of this water supply were the duties of the Pant Masters who were elected to office at vestry meetings of St Nicholas' church. The site of the old well-head is now clearly marked.

Much of the Market Place as Hutchinson saw it was to disappear in the mid-19th century. The old Norman church of St Nicholas, the town church built by Bishop Flambard, long-connected with the old city guilds, was described in 1787 as being 'very plain and meanly built, being constructed of small and perishable stones, so that from frequent pointing it is now almost covered in mortar'. It was rebuilt by the zealous Victorians. Next to the church stood a house called New Place or the Bull's Head, built during the Middle Ages as a palace for the Nevilles of Raby and Brancepeth, the Earls of Westmorland. In its prime, this was an extensive property extending some way up Claypath with gardens running down to the river. After his

41. Restored statue of Neptune, the Market Place.

involvement in the Rebellion of the North, 1569, planned at Raby Castle, the Earl forfeited this property to the Crown. It was eventually bought from King James II in 1612 by Henry Smith's Charity and used as a factory, a workhouse and charity school before it, too, was demolished, the last evidence of it disappearing in 1853. The school concerned, the Blue Coat school, was founded in 1708, originally teaching just six boys. By 1732 it contained 30 boys and 20 girls; in 1812 it moved to a new site in Claypath.

The architect of the present St Nicholas' church, the parish church of the city, was J. F. Pritchett of Darlington. Built between 1857 and 1858 to a neo-Gothic design and occupying the entire north side of the Market Place, it was the first church in the city to be adorned with a spire and was called in the national press of the time 'the most beautiful specimen of church architecture in the north of England'. Pritchett had not originally been engaged to build a completely new church. The old building had undergone extensive, often makeshift, repairs over the centuries and had even suffered the ignominy of being almost hidden from view by a piazza built in front of almost the whole of its south face during the 18th century. This piazza was used subsequently as a corn-market before being removed in 1854. During the first half of the 19th century, all sorts of schemes were devised and costed to continue the repairs of the old church but it was realised in 1857 that such piecemeal efforts were doing no good at all and it was decided that a new church had to be built. Generous financial assistance from the new incumbent, George Townshend Fox, and a donation of

£1,000 from the Marchioness of Londonderry did much to bring about this decision. J. F. Pritchett revised his designs and added a steeple to them. When this was felt to be too expensive an addition, Mr. Fox donated the required extra £300. The interior of St Nicholas' church as it is today would be quite alien to Messrs. Pritchett and Fox for there was a great deal of work undertaken to change it completely by 1981. The architect of the modernisation was Ronald Sims. The old pews are gone, while new and tasteful wooden balconies containing offices and vestry now stand where once there was just useless space. The body of the church (the nave and north aisle) is now one large multi-functional room with a movable altar area; the old chancel has been screened off to form a small chapel. The whole is most pleasing and a credit to all who laboured so long and hard to raise the money to allow such a project to be undertaken.

Between St Nicholas' church and the Town Hall is an alley whose position once saved the life of an arrogant archbishop. In 1283, just a few weeks after the death of the Bishop of Durham, Robert de Insula, Archbishop Wickwane of York travelled to Durham to claim, not for the first time, that he had 'rights of visitation' there. On attempting to enter the cathedral, he was refused admission and made his way down to the Market Place and the church of St Nicholas. Gaining entrance, he mounted into the pulpit and began to excommunicate the Durham monks. On hearing of the archbishop's presence in the city, and the reasons for it, a band of angry citizens gathered at the church. So afraid was Wickwane that he fled in terror, but the mob had not been idle while they hastened his departure; one of his horse's ears was cut off. The prelate's life was saved only by the intervention of one of the king's commissioners who was present and who diverted the attention of the angry crowd while Wickwane sped off along Walkergate to the comparative safety of nearby Kepier Hospital. Walkergate, it should be mentioned, indicates yet another Durham connection with the medieval guilds, 'walkers' having been fullers or cloth merchants.

Next to St Nicholas' church, on the west side of the Market Place are the city's main civic buildings. The old Town Hall, known as the Guildhall, dates from the time of King Edward III, having been built in 1356. In 1535 Bishop Tunstall caused it to be considerably rebuilt before giving it to the city. Further rebuilding was undertaken subsequently by Bishop Cosin in 1665, and other major alterations were made in 1752. It appears that more rebuilding was carried out in the mid-1750s. Of considerable historical interest is the Guildhall's association with the old city guilds, some of which still exist and meet in this old building. The arms of many of these can still be seen there. Medieval in origin, the guilds were jealous guardians of their privileges. Their main functions were to oversee and guarantee the maintenance of high standards of workmanship in their craft and to ensure, as far as possible, a monopoly of work for their members. They also supervised, and carefully, the admission of new apprentices to the craft, monitoring their long progress to full membership. Scotsmen were not admitted. Sometimes the guilds undertook the provision of pensions for elderly or infirm members and assisted with funeral arrangements. Between the years 1450 and 1667, although some could well have been established much earlier, the craft and merchant guilds of the City of Durham were as follows:

Weavers and Websters	1450
Cordwainers	1458
Barber surgeons, Waxmakers, Ropers and Stringers	1468
Skinners and Glovers	1507
Butchers	1520
Goldsmiths, Plumbers, Pewterers, Potters, Painters, Glaziers and Tin Plate Workers	1532
Barkers and Tanners	1547
Drapers and Tailors	1549
Merchants or Mercers (incorporating Grocers 1345, Mercers 1393, Salters 1394, Ironmongers 1464 and Haberdashers 1467)	1561
Fullers and Feltmakers	1565
Curriers and Tallow Chandlers	1570
Free Masons, Rough Masons, Wallers, Slaters, Paviours, Plasterers and Bricklayers	1594
Blacksmiths, Lorimers, Locksmiths, Cutlers, Bladesmiths and Girdlers	1610
Saddlers and Upholsterers	1659
Carpenters, Joiners, Wheelwrights, Sawyers and Coopers	1661
Dyers and Listers	1667

All guild members had to take part in the annual celebration of the Feast of Corpus Christi which took place on the Thursday after Trinity Sunday. This was one of Durham's great days when Town and Church came together. A record of one such procession was made in the late 16th century by a servant of the cathedral who remembered the days before the Dissolution of the Abbeys in 1539. He records that:

On that day the Town Bailiff would stand upon the Toll Booth in the Market Place and summon all the various guilds of trades and professions to get out their banners and torches and go to the north door of the Cathedral where they would form a line, banners to the west and torches on the east side of the path as far as Windy Gap. In the church of St Nicholas there was a fine shrine called the Corpus Christi shrine which was carried in the procession. It was well gilded and had on its top a square container of crystal in which the sacrament was kept. Four priests carried it up to Palace Green, preceded by a procession of people from all the churches in the town, until it came to rest at Windy Gap. Then St Cuthbert's Banner and two crosses led the procession of Prior and monks from the Cathedral to where it stood. Then the whole community, together with the choir knelt and prayed before the shrine. After the Prior had censed it, it was carried before the Prior, community and choir into the Cathedral where it was set up in the Choir. There followed a solemn service with the Te Deum sung, accompanied by the organ. All the guild banners followed the procession into the Cathedral where they processed round St. Cuthbert's Feretory, their torches burning throughout the service. After the service the shrine was carried in procession back to St. Nicholas Church followed by all the banners. The shrine was then kept in the church vestry until the next year.

The shrine itself was destroyed by one Dr. Harvey, a commissioner during the Commonwealth, who was sent to the city for that specific purpose. He trod on it and it fell to pieces! Also on Corpus Christi Day, members of the various guilds performed plays on Palace Green, plays, it must be assumed, since they are no longer extant, similar in style and content to the famous York mystery plays. The Corpus Christi Guild was eventually abolished by King Edward VI but the ceremony itself lived on. After the Restoration of King Charles II, the Guild Procession took place annually on 29 May, known as Restoration or Oak Apple Day, and was continued until about 1770. The yearly blessing of the colliery banners in the cathedral is perceived by some as a modern folk legacy of that great medieval Guild Procession.

On view in the Guildhall is the plate of Durham City Council and of the guilds. Much of the City plate was presented by Bishop Lord Crewe. The mayor's 44-in. long chain, of 18-carat gold, was bought by public subscription and presented to the City in 1870.

By the middle of the 19th century, the Guildhall had ceased to be a suitable building, or large enough, to accommodate all the business transacted by the City, so in 1850 a new town hall was proposed by the then mayor, William Henderson, and built onto the rear of the old structure. Public subscription was called for again, and in 1851 the Main Hall, as it is called, was opened. The London architect Philip Charles Hardwick designed the new hall to be a less complicated and smaller-scale version of Westminster Hall. The hammer-beam roof is most impressive, as is the great west window which includes portrayals of the Corpus Christi procession, four bishops of Durham, the arms of several local families and a scene centred around King Edward III on horseback in Durham Market Place. Another stained-glass window is dedicated to the men of the Durham Light Infantry. The imposing fireplace is of Prudhoe stone. A fine collection of paintings adorns the wall of the Main Hall, many of them by Clement Burlison, an acclaimed artist whose father had been a businessman in Silver Street. When Burlison died in 1899, his bequest of paintings formed the basis for the City Art Gallery, known as the Burlison Gallery and sited in the Guildhall complex. Burlison was known for his high quality portrait painting and for producing excellent copies of pictures which hung in European art galleries. His work was often exhibited at London's Royal Academy.

A plaque near the Town Hall's main doors records some of the deeds of one of Durham's sons. He was Granville Sharp, born in the city in 1735 and an indefatigable fighter against slavery. It was largely due to his constant campaigning that slavery was made illegal in Britain in 1772. Co-founder and first chairman of the British and Foreign Bible Society, he died in London in 1813.

The most striking feature of the Mayor's Chamber, sometimes called the Old Council Room, is a Jacobean-style oak fire-place. It came originally from a building in the North Bailey but before it was presented to the city, two panel portraits, one of King Charles I and the other of his wife, Queen Henrietta Maria, were removed. These were said to be copies of originals by Van Dyck and were later claimed to be originals, but this is not the case. The panels were restored to their rightful setting in the fireplace in 1865. Also on display in this complex of buildings are some of the possessions, including the violin, of one of Durham's most famous inhabitants, the Polish dwarf Count Joseph Boruwlaski, who lived in Durham probably from 1822 to 1837. He is buried inside the cathedral near the north door.

After World War II there was reconstruction of parts of the Town Hall complex to create a supper room and offices. The Tourist Information Office can be found on the ground floor of the Town Hall in the Market Place, while at the south end of the frontage is the *Market Tavern*.

Beneath the Town Hall is Durham's covered market, a large subterranean area open to shoppers on Thursday, Friday and Saturday. It is an Aladdin's cave of stalls and arcade shops selling articles of every description. A pork butcher here is famed for his pease pudding, while old gramophone records recall memories of earlier hit parades. Engraved glass, watches and their batteries, fresh fish, antiquarian books, budgerigars and bird seed are just some of the commodities available. Durham also has an outside market, selling predominantly fruit and vegetables, flowers and fabric on Saturdays.

Dating essentially from the middle of the 18th century are 21 and 25 Market Place; mid-19th century are nos. 14, 16, 22-23 and the attractive four-storey 'round corner' of no. 11. Its shop dates from 1870. There are three substantially built banks in the Market Place. The National Westminster, designed by Gibson, dates from 1876; Barclays, by A. Waterhouse, was built in 1887 and extended in 1924; while Lloyds, in the baroque style, was erected in about 1900.

Chapter Seven

Saddler Street and Owengate

It is probably not generally realised what an enormous debt epicures and thespians owe to the City of Durham, and to Saddler Street in particular. It was here that mustard was first manufactured in England and that 'theatre' gained not one but two solid footholds in the north country. Saddler Street or, more properly, Fleshergate leading into Saddler Street, is a narrow, medieval thoroughfare, the route from Market Place to the cathedral and to the Baileys, the former the religious heart of the city, the latter the 18th-century social heart.

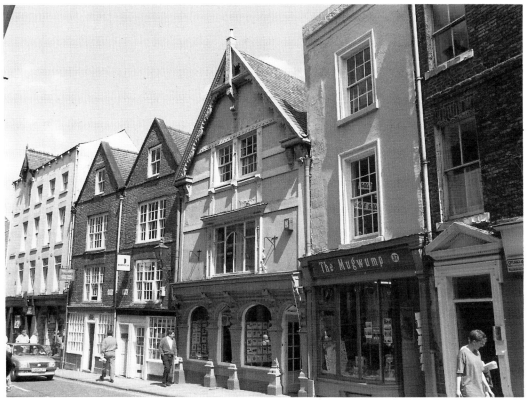

42.   Saddler Street.

Fleshergate derives its name from the fact that this was the area where butchers plied their trade. There were complaints during the 18th century about the way some of them butchered animals in the street outside their shops, causing considerable distress to passers-by, let alone to the animals. In the 16th century, what is now no. 79, on the right, leaving Market Place, was probably the home of Sir Richard Saddler. Concealed by the present exterior is the building's original timber frame. This is the oldest house in the street.

Just along the path on the same side a large, early 19th-century teapot, originally from Claypath, hangs out over the narrow pavement from nos. 73-75. In the mid-19th century it hung over C. F. White's shop in Market Place, was then moved to the grocery shop of Miss White and Mrs. Vasey at 30 Gilesgate, and next travelled to the grocery business of James Fowler in Claypath. These Saddler Street premises should be a place of pilgrimage for all who like the flavour of their meat enhanced by good biting English mustard, for it was in the 18th-century mill to the rear of this property that one Mrs. Clements, or Clemens, reputedly first ground mustard seeds to create Durham mustard in 1720. In its day this was famed throughout the land, and King George II is said to have been one of its keenest users. So popular was the product that many local farmers took to growing mustard as a main crop to supply the mill. One such farm was Houghall, at Shincliffe, now an agricultural and horticultural college. The product is commemorated in an old Durham saying:

> The City of Durham is famous for seven things
> Wood, Water and Pleasant Walks, Law and Gospel,
> Old Maids and Mustard.

Other sources suggest, however, that Durham mustard was first manufactured in 1692. There were eventually three mustard factories in Durham: William Ainsley's was in Saddler Street and then Waddington Street; John Balmbrough's occupied a site at the foot of Silver Street; while Simpson and Willan operated in Gilesgate. Colman's bought the last of these factories in 1897. The steep steps which descend from Saddler Street towards Elvet Bridge are known as the Magdalen Steps. The gabled property, nos. 34-35, dates from the 18th century and was once the *Bee Hive Inn*.

Many of the buildings in Saddler Street conceal their true age for behind many of the more modern façades lie timber-framed shops and dwellings, some properties still retaining very old staircases and fine examples of plastering and woodwork. Sadly, not much of this is visible to the visitor today. It is, nevertheless, interesting to note that these features still exist in Durham and are protected by law. A sharp turn after the sandstone columns of no. 64 and before the *Shakespeare Inn* leads the traveller back in time along a vennel. This one, connecting Saddler Street with Silver Street, follows the old line of the castle moat, hence the name Moatside Lane, It is arguable, though, that the vennel was originally 'Motte-side' Lane, deriving its appellation from the fact that the castle is built on a 'motte' or hill.

A little further up Saddler Street but on the opposite side of the road, another vennel leads steeply down to the river. This is Drury Lane and, as might be suspected,

ESTABLISHED 1692.

AINSLEY'S CELEBRATED DURHAM MUSTARD,

MANUFACTURED SOLELY AT THE ORIGINAL ESTABLISHMENT,

22, FOOT OF SILVER-STREET, DURHAM,

BY

JOHN BALMBROUGH,

Sole Proprietor and only Successor to the late Joseph William Ainsley (and to the Business for so many years carried on by his present wife, then Eleanor Ainsley, and who is the last and only survivor of the Family of Joseph Wm. Ainsley, who first manufactured the Article.]

THE Nobility, Clergy, Gentry, and Inhabitants generally of Durham and its vicinity, are respectfully informed that the above CELEBRATED MUSTARD is made from the finest selected Samples of English Brown Seed, on the principles which first gave to Durham its celebrity for the Article, combined with every Improvement which science has since developed. The greatest skill and attention is observed in the preparation of the Seed, which is desiccated in a manner known only to the above Proprietor, whereby all its great strength, aromatic flavour, and strong piquant qualities are retained. It is warranted to be free from every adulteration, such as Turmeric and other chemical preparations, and, to prove it, analyzation is at all times invited.

Sold Wholesale and Retail in Bottles, Bladders and Casks ; and, to protect the Public from being imposed upon, each Label with the Bottles, Bladders, &c., will have upon it a representation of Durham Cathedral and the City Ams, together with the Signature of the Proprietor, and without which it is not GENUINE.

☞ CAUTION.—The great celebrity this Mustard has gained for itself, both here and abroad, has been the means of inducing several unscrupulous, and unprincipled parties of the Name of " AINSLEY" to attempt to impose on the public a SPURIOUS ARTICLE pretended to be manufactured from original receipts, &c. It is therefore considered necessary to state that these parties have not the slightest connexion with the above Old Established Business.

OBSERVE THE ORIGINAL MANUFACTORY,

22, FOOT OF SILVER STREET, DURHAM.

Jno Balmbrough

SOLE PROPRIETOR.

43.   Victorian advertisement for Durham mustard.

it has theatrical connections. Behind 43 and 44 Saddler Street there was a theatre from 1722 until at least the end of the century, while, diagonally opposite, behind no. 61, another theatre existed from 1792. This survived, although much changed and used latterly as a warehouse, into the middle of the 20th century. There was another theatre in Hallgarth Street in 1760. The first of the two Saddler Street theatres, behind nos. 43 and 44, existed in 1722 when it was described as 'a very handsome Play-house built fit for the Reception of Quality and Gentry'. In 1746 the property was listed as having, 'a Cock-Pit and Playhouse'. In 1754, John Richardson leased the site and eventually built a new theatre there, which was opened on 10 July 1771. John Sykes records that:

> The new theatre in the city of Durham was opened with *The West Indian*, and other entertainments, to a very genteel audience, who expressed the greatest satisfaction at the elegance of the house, and of the performance in general.

One of the players at this theatre was James Cawdell who, in 1782, became manager of the company which acted here. When he was refused permission to continue to lease the property, he decided to build a new and larger theatre just across Saddler Street. It was opened in grand style:

> 6th July, 1791 – The foundation stone of a new theatre was laid in the city of Durham with great masonic eclat by George Finch, esq., deputy grand master for the county, in the presence of Thomas Chipchase, esq., mayor, and William Ambler, esq., recorder of the city. A plate, with a suitable inscription, was deposited within the stone.

The building was obviously erected fairly quickly because the next entry about the new theatre records that on:

> March 12th, 1792, this theatre was opened with an occasional prelude, called *Apollo's Holiday*, written by Mr. Cawdell; the new comedy of *Wild Oats*; and the farce of *The Spoiled Child*.

Mr. Cawdell used his talents as a writer for the public good; on 22 March 1793, in order to help to raise funds for the new Durham Infirmary:

> the tragedy of Cato was represented at the theatre, Durham, to assist the funds of this institution; the parts of Cato and Juba being performed by W. Eddis and W. Smith esqrs., of that city, which characters they supported throughout with great success. An excellent prologue was written for the occasion by Mr. Cawdell, the manager, and admirably delivered by him. The house was full in every part, and the sum of fifty guineas was paid into the hands of the treasurer of the Infirmary.

Cawdell died at his house in the South Bailey in 1800, and the theatre he had built was leased from then until 1806 to Stephen Kemble, undoubtedly the most illustrious name associated with the Durham theatre. He was a member of the great 18th-century acting family, and brother to Charles and John Philip Kemble. Their

44. Durham Theatre poster advertising *Chapter of Accidents* and *Rosina*, 1796. Reproduced by permission of Durham University Library.

45. Theatre Royal poster, 1859. Reproduced by permission of Durham University Library.

sister was the famous Mrs. Siddons, who occasionally appeared in the Durham
theatre while Stephen was managing it. Stephen's wife was an actress and their
daughter, Fanny, was at one time the toast of London because of her beauty, the
charming songs she composed and the way she sang them. Fanny, who already had
the fame, found her fortune when she married the son of Richard Arkwright, that
same Richard Arkwright who, in 1769, developed spinning which used water power,
and so contributed to the Industrial Revolution.

Stephen Kemble died on 6 June 1822. Sykes records:

Died, at the Grove, near Durham, in his 64th year, Stephen George Kemble, esq.,
the celebrated comedian, and formerly manager of the theatres-royal of Newcastle,
Glasgow, and Edinburgh. Mr. Kemble, who was a very corpulent man, had retired for
some years from the exercise of the laborious profession of an actor. In many characters
he was confessedly unrivalled; and it is no small commendation that he was considered
by the late Mr. Sheridan to be the best declaimer he had ever heard on or off the stage.
He was also possessed of considerable literary talents.

46. Durham jail.

On 11 June, his remains were buried in the Chapel of the Nine Altars in the cathedral.

Just two years earlier, in 1820, the old north gateway which straddled Saddler street and which stood between nos. 49 and 50 had been taken down. It had been the city gaol and was an extremely strong structure, its lower part having been defended by both a gate and a portcullis. It was the last of the city gates to be removed. A 14th-century bastion and part of the old city wall can still be seen to the rear of no. 50.

The gateway, often referred to as the gaol gate, was first used as a prison in 1424 on the order of Cardinal Langley, who could no longer bear to see prisoners badly-housed in the cellars of the castle. Records suggest that their lot was not greatly improved by the move, and certainly their gaolers were an unsavoury lot. A report on conditions in Durham Gaol in 1774 includes the following observations:

> The debtors have two damp, unhealthy rooms, 10 ft. 4 inches square. No sewers. At more than one of my visits I learned that the dirt, ashes etc. had lain there many months. The felons are put at night into dungeons; one 7 ft. square for three prisoners; another, the great hole, 16 ½ft. by 12, has only a little window. In this I saw six prisoners chained to the floor. In that situation they had been for many weeks, and were very sick. The straw on the floor was almost worn to dust. Commonside debtors in the low jail, whom I saw eating boiled bread and water, told me this was the only nourishment some had lived on for nearly twelve months. At several of my visits there were boys, thirteen and fifteen years of age, confined with the most profligate and abandoned.

The gate was an impediment to traffic since it only allowed for the passage of traffic in one direction at a time, and in 1773 all vehicles were stopped when the long-unused portcullis descended unexpectedly during repairs to the building. So heavily did it come down that it embedded itself deeply in the roadway and had to be cut to pieces to allow traffic to flow again.

Royal Mail coaches calling at Durham on their way from London to Edinburgh had to negotiate the narrow Saddler Street and the even more constricting North Gate as they made their way to the *Red Lion Inn*, which stood in the Bailey on the site now occupied by Hatfield College. The coach drivers must have been very relieved when the old prison was removed. It was last used as a prison in August 1819; by then the new gaol was ready at the end of Old Elvet. Even today traffic finds Saddler Street a difficult highway. There is barely room for two cars to pass and, even given the assistance of traffic lights, the wise motorist will park his car before negotiating this ancient street.

Durham art gallery used to be housed at 49 Saddler Street, a property which, since 1925, has been the Salvation Army citadel. Parts of the medieval building are incorporated into the present fabric. At the beginning of the 19th century it was converted to use as assembly rooms. Almost directly opposite, 50 Saddler Street served the city during Victorian times as a subscription news room and library. Again, part of the medieval fabric of the gateway can be seen in the cellar. At the head of Saddler Street, routes diverge. One, a continuation of the highway, becomes the Bailey, while a turn to the right leads through Owengate to Palace Green.

It is perhaps anticipation of the first sight of the cathedral which causes so many travellers to negotiate the short Owengate without giving its buildings a second glance. No. 5 is, nevertheless, particularly worthy of note, essentially a timber-framed building dating from the 16th century. No. 7 is an almshouse, originally founded by Bishop Cosin in 1666 on Palace Green; the present building dates from 1838 but is in the Tudor style. Nos. 2 and 4 were built at the end of the 18th century while no. 3 predates them by 100 years.

What is particularly fascinating about Fleshergate, Saddler Street and Owengate is that, bottleneck though they be, they have, for almost 1,000 years, without the assistance of town-planners or tourist officers, funnelled pilgrims and tourists effortlessly towards their goal – Durham Cathedral.

Chapter Eight

The Baileys and the College

The long and elegant road which leads from Saddler Street to the Water Gate and Prebends' Bridge is generally called the Bailey but is, in fact, the North and South Bailey. The demarcation line between the end of Saddler Street and the start of the North Bailey was for centuries the medieval North Gate, demolished in 1820.

Property in the Bailey area was owned in the medieval period by those whose business was the manning and maintenance of the castle, but by the 17th century new properties were being built there, to house people who had no connection with military matters. The Baileys had become the fashionable place to live, just far enough out of the city centre for residents not to be troubled by the hurly-burly of traffic, trade and business but close enough to be convenient for the shops and other facilities when they were needed. Nor was proximity to the cathedral a social disadvantage. Certainly, by the 18th century a visit to the great church was, for many, not so much prompted by a desire to worship as to be seen in Sunday finery chatting to the people 'who mattered'. The content of the sermon and the quality of the choir's singing were, to such people, secondary considerations compared with their concern about the proximity of their seats in the cathedral to those of the rich, famous or influential.

Several people of note have lived in the Bailey, some notable purely in a local context, others known further afield. The influential architect Ignatius Bonomi (1787-1870) lived in Durham for more than 40 years, some of that time in 5 North Bailey. Bonomi was of Italian stock, his father Guiseppe, also an architect, having been persuaded to leave Florence to work for Robert Adam in England, where he arrived in 1767. Here he remained, apart from a brief visit to Italy in 1783-84. The family home was in London and Guiseppe Bonomi achieved moderate fame, even being mentioned by Jane Austen in *Sense and Sensibility*.

In 1803, Ignatius Bonomi joined the family business to train as an architect. His father died in 1808 and Ignatius decided to carry on the family practice. In 1813, having done some work in North Yorkshire, principally at Skelton Castle, he was successful in his application to be appointed as County Bridge Surveyor for Durham; this meant that his home almost had to be in County Durham and Bonomi chose Durham City as his base. In 1837, aged 50, Bonomi married Charlotte Anne Fielding; the wedding took place first in an Anglican church, Charlotte Anne being the daughter of a Church of England clergyman, but they were married again a few days later in St Cuthbert's Roman Catholic church in Durham City. Ignatius was, at this time, a Roman Catholic and St Cuthbert's was one of the churches of which he had been the architect some years earlier.

Until this time, Bonomi had lived in a house he had designed himself, Elvet Hill, but he and his new bride moved into 5 North Bailey which had, until then, been

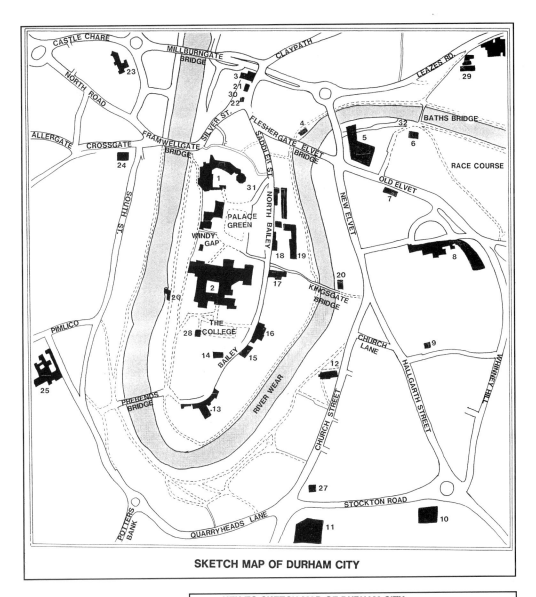

SKETCH MAP OF DURHAM CITY

KEY TO SKETCH MAP OF DURHAM CITY

1	DURHAM CASTLE	17	ST CHAD'S COLLEGE
2	DURHAM CATHEDRAL	18	HERITAGE CENTRE
3	ST GILES' CHURCH	19	HATFIELD COLLEGE
4	BROWN'S BOATHOUSE	20	DUNELM HOUSE
5	ROYAL COUNTRY HOTEL	21	STATUE OF MARQUESS OF LONDONDERRY
6	SWIMMING BATHS	22	STATUE OF NEPTUNE
7	OLD SHIRE HALL	23	ARTS CENTRE
8	COURTS AND DURHAM PRISON	24	ST MARGARET'S CHURCH
9	MEDIAEVAL TITHE BARN	25	DURHAM SCHOOL
10	UNIVERSITY LIBRARY	26	MUSEUM OF ARCHAEOLOGY
11	UNIVERSITY SCIENCE LABORATORIES	27	NEW INN
12	ST OSWALD'S CHURCH	28	CHORISTER SCHOOL
13	ST CUTHBERT'S SOCIETY	29	UNIVERSITY SCHOOL OF EDUCATION
14	ST MARY-THE-LESS	30	MARKET PLACE
15	BOWES HOUSE	31	OWENGATE
16	ST JOHN'S COLLEGE	32	ELVET WATERSIDE

47. Sketch map of Durham
city, (drawn by Adrian Perrett).

occupied by Charlotte Anne and her sister Sophy, who continued to live with them. The two ladies had run a school there. Bonomi's office was, conveniently, almost opposite at 45 North Bailey. He was County Bridge Surveyor for 37 years, retiring from the post in 1850 at the age of 63. He did not give up work but continued with his private practice. In 1856 the Bonomis went to live in London, where Charlotte Anne died in 1860. Ignatius Bonomi died at his Wimbledon home, The Camels, which he had designed himself, in 1870.

The original 7 North Bailey, replaced in 1966 by a new university building, was once owned by a remarkable character called John Gully. He died at this elegant home in 1863, in his 80th year, having moved into the city because of his frailty. A look at his later life and his vast circle of influential friends gives no hint of his modest beginning. Before the end of his first year in business the young Gully had been languishing in gaol, imprisoned for debt. The story of how he rose from bankruptcy and obscurity to become a member of parliament as well as an exceedingly wealthy colliery owner and keeper of racehorses reads almost like something from Grimms' fairy tales.

John Gully was born at Wick in Gloucestershire in 1783; his parents kept the *Crown Inn* there. While he was still young the family moved to Bristol where his father traded as a butcher until his death, which occurred before John had attained his majority. Mrs. Gully carried on the business until her son was 21, when she handed it over to him. It was soon obvious to the young man that she had not been a good businesswoman and that the books did not balance. For his mother's ineptitude, John Gully was convicted of debt and consigned to the King's Bench Prison. Here he found he had plenty of time to exercise, for as well as plying his trade as a butcher before awaiting His Majesty's pleasure, he had begun to find considerable local fame as a pugilist, a bare-knuckle boxer. Word of Gully's imprisonment soon reached the ears of England's then-champion boxer, the 'Game Chicken', Henry Pearce, who visited him in gaol. In the afternoon a bout was arranged between them. It was a good-humoured affair but both men threw some good and heavy punches, Gully having no need to be ashamed of his performance. He felt that, given time and training, he would be able to beat Pearce. A patron of boxing named Fletcher Reid heard about the prison bout and wanted to see the two men meet properly in the prize ring; therefore he paid off Gully's debts and sent him to Virginia Water to be trained.

Although John Gully was almost six feet tall and of an athletic build, he did not look like a typical boxer. His greatest strengths were his courage and confidence in his ability. The fight with Pearce eventually took place at Hailsham in Sussex in October 1805. Some of the greatest patrons of the sport were present that day, including the Duke of Clarence, later King William IV. After 64 rounds of a fight which lasted for one hour seventeen minutes, Gully conceded defeat, but Pearce admitted that it was the hardest fight he had ever had. When he retired from the ring, Pearce handed over his title to John Gully. It was two years before any challenger for the title came forward; Gully's opponent was a Mr. Gregson and the fight went to 36 rounds. At the end of this both men, not surprisingly, had difficulty standing. One beating by Gully should have been enough for any man but six months later Gregson came back for more. This time, in May 1808, it took the champion just 28 rounds to defeat him. The crowd which turned up to see this bout was enormous, quite incredible considering that the fight was supposed to be a secret. Having suggested to Gregson that he should retire from the ring, Gully climbed into Lord Barrymore's carriage and was driven to the tavern he owned by then in Carey Street, in London's Lincoln's Inn Fields.

Soon afterwards, Gully himself retired from boxing and, for the next few years, devoted his time to tavern-keeping. He did, nevertheless, find time to cultivate a much more lucrative interest. He loved horse-racing and was either clever or lucky with the bets he placed, because he made so much money gambling that he soon had enough to buy Hare Park in Hertfordshire, and then Ackworth Park in Yorkshire. Here he mixed with the gentry. Gully had made his mark, was making money and was enjoying life to the full as a country landowner. He had come a long way from debtors' prison. John Gully was intelligent, good-humoured and kind; he was readily accepted by his new friends. He never tried to hide his past but answered honestly questions about his early life. He continued to pursue his racing interests and kept permanent lodgings at Newmarket. Soon his reputation as a racehorse-breeder and proprietor brought him to the notice of one of the foremost betting men in the land, His Royal Highness the Prince Regent, later King George IV. Gully became his racing adviser and continued to breed some of the finest racehorses of the time; his horses won the Derby three times, the Oaks, the St Leger and the Two Thousand Guineas. On two famous occasions he lost £40,000 and £85,000, but later recouped these losses. In 1854 his net winnings were just short of £11,000, a phenomenal sum for those days.

In 1832 Gully had been elected Member of Parliament for Pontefract which he represented as a Liberal. His time in the House of Commons was devoted largely to supporting the campaign which sought to curb wasteful public expenditure. His speeches were neither many nor brilliant but what he did say was timely and sensible. The most peculiar aspect of Gully's time at Westminster was that he had never had any ambition to be there; he had stood for election merely to win a bet!

Apart from his skills as a prize-fighter and breeder of superb racehorses, John Gully is best remembered as a colliery-owner. He gradually withdrew from his gambling pursuits and so avoided the bankruptcy which befell so many of his friends. The lilac coat he always wore on the racecourse was seen less and less as he invested more of his time in land and coalmines in the north of England. He bought shares in the Hetton Coal Company at a time when geologists were saying that to attempt to work any of the projected seams would be crass folly. The geologists were wrong and Gully hung on to his shares, watching as they increased in value. Next he joined forces with Sir William Chaytor and together they financed the sinking of collieries at Thornley. He also had a large interest in the Trimdon collieries, but in 1862 he sold his shares in them to buy the Wingate Grange estate along with its collieries, and these Gully retained until his death. Just before his purchase of Wingate John Gully was living in Hampshire, but he then moved to Cocken Hall near Durham. He was buried, however, near one of his former homes, close to Pontefract. Gully married twice and fathered 24 children. He had started out in life with a little money, had lost it all through no fault of his own, and had gone on to find fame and fortune. The story of John Gully is truly a tale of rags to riches.

Hatfield College, founded in 1846 and named after the great 14th-century Bishop of Durham, Thomas Hatfield, is housed in a collection of buildings ranging in date from the mid-18th to the mid-20th century. It should be remembered that although the Stockton and Darlington Railway was the first (in 1825) in the world to carry passengers, for several years thereafter coaches continued to be one of the main modes of travel. Where coaches stopped there were coaching inns, and one of these was the *Red Lion*, now part of Hatfield College. The college chapel was built in 1853. The Assembly Rooms just across the road from Hatfield College are now most frequently used as a university theatre, but were in former days a gathering and dancing place.

On the same side of the road as Hatfield and at the North Bailey's junction with Bow Lane stands the church of St Mary-le-Bow, said to have been built on the site of the shelter which first housed Cuthbert's body when it was brought to Durham. The church has not been used as such since 1967 and was converted into a heritage centre in 1976. The south wall of the church formed part of the inner bailey. Part of the medieval church and the old bailey gateway collapsed in 1637, but the rebuilding of the church was not started until about 1671, finishing in 1685. The tower was erected in 1702. This building is well worth a visit, not only for its excellent exhibitions but also for the superb 17th- and 18th-century woodwork still retained there. The narrow, cobbled Bow Lane itself leads from the North Bailey through the remains of the outer bailey walls to

48. St Mary-le-Bow, North Bailey.

Kingsgate Bridge, for pedestrians only, and across to Dunelm House and New Elvet. Kingsgate Bridge was designed in 1962 by Ove Arup and Partners. During the 16th century, the river was spanned here by Bow Bridge and, before that, by a ford. It was down Bow Lane that William the Conqueror fled, crossing the wear by a ford and not stopping, it is said, until he reached the safety of North Yorkshire on the other side of the River Tees, well out of St Cuthbert's grasp. The reason for his flight was that, having insisted that Cuthbert's coffin should be opened so that he could see for himself the uncorrupt body, he was seized by a strange illness and could not leave the great church quickly enough. He was sure that he would not be safe from Cuthbert's wrath until he was out of the patrimony.

On the corner of Bow Lane, a site now occupied by part of St Chad's College, there used to stand a cottage which was the home until 1780 of the Porter family, the most famous of whom were Jane, Robert and Anna Maria. Although all were born in Durham they found fame, it must be admitted, after the family left the city. Jane was wont to rise very early every morning and as a child read Spenser's *Faerie Queene*. She loved to write and, because she always seemed to be deep in thought, was often called La Penserosa. Her first novel was *Thaddeus of Warsaw*, a historical novel published in 1803 when Jane was twenty-seven. In 1810 she chronicled the life of William Wallace in *The Scottish Chiefs*, a novel banned in France on the order of Napoleon. She also found success with her stories *The Pastor's Fireside* and *The Field of Forty Footsteps* as well as collaborating with her sister Anna Maria in 1824 to produce *Tales Round a Winter's Hearth*. Anna Maria was, like Jane, educated in Edinburgh, where a frequent visitor to the house was Walter Scott. Nicknamed L'Allegra because of her ever-cheerful disposition, she was just 13 when she started to write *Artless Tales* published two years later, but she is best remembered for her novel of the French Revolutionary war, *The Hungarian Brothers*. Anna Maria and Jane's brother was to become Sir Robert Ker Porter to whom there is a monument in Bristol Cathedral. He was an artist and a writer as well as being a bon viveur, a generally dashing character and friend of both Scott and Turner. He fought at the Battle of Corunna, married a Russian princess, was honoured by the Shah of Persia and knighted by not only the Prince Regent but also the kings of Sweden and Wurttemberg.

Just across the Bailey from Bow Lane, Dun Cow Lane leads to Palace Green and to the cathedral itself. There are several attractive houses in the North Bailey as it makes its way towards the entrance to one of Durham's most peaceful places, the College, its gateway marking the start of the South Bailey. The present early 16th-century gateway, with an upper room which used to be St Helen's Chapel, replaced the much earlier entrance to the monastery. It is in this part of the city that the supernatural enters the Durham story for it is said that nos. 23 and 24 North Bailey, built on the site of the monastery's almonry, are haunted, one by a group of children accompanied by an elderly lady, the other by a man clad in a nightgown and cap. No. 1 South Bailey occupies the site of the monastery's almonry school whose children, some 30 of them, performed as choristers in the lady chapel.

To leave the Bailey and walk through Prior Castell's College gateway into the quiet college itself, a green surrounded by buildings, is to step back into the late 18th or early 19th century. Here is a house now occupied by the Dean but formerly by the

49. Kingsgate Bridge and the cathedral from Dunelm House.

50. Bow Lane, from steps of Kingsgate bridge.

Prior; tucked away in a corner is the world-famous Chorister School and all around are buildings which praise the glories of a bygone age. It was in this area that Oliver Cromwell planned to establish Durham's first university. On the green itself stands an eight-sided conduit or well-house, a reservoir erected in 1751. Also octagonal in shape is the 14th-century Prior's Kitchen. The terrace of houses opposite the Deanery is intrinsically Georgian but the foundations are much older, some dating back to the 14th century. The Chorister School has for centuries provided young singers for the cathedral choir and continues to do so. Also educated here are boys who are not especially blessed with a talent for singing but whose parents favour this type of public school education. Nos. 3 and 4 South Bailey are both properties which used to have strong county connections. No. 3 was built in the mid-18th century by Sir Robert Eden, and it was later owned by William Henderson, one of the owners of the Durham carpet factory. Durham Girls' High School was founded here in 1884. Later the school moved to Leazes House in Claypath, one-time home of the other owner of the carpet factory and Member of Parliament, John Henderson. No. 4, Bowes House, again 18th-century, was once home to some of the Bowes family and, in particular, to an ancestor of Queen Elizabeth the Queen Mother, Mary Eleanor Bowes, who married the Earl of Strathmore. One owner of the house was the great-grandmother of Henry George Liddell. Born in 1811 at Binchester, near Bishop Auckland, Henry George Liddell went on to become Headmaster of Winchester College and then Dean of Christ Church. He is most famous for having compiled, with Robert Scott, the Greek lexicon which bears their names. The famous *Alice In Wonderland* was Liddell's daughter because it was for her that Charles Lutwidge Dodgson, or Lewis Carroll, wrote the original 'Alice' story. Dodgson and Liddell knew each other well since both worked at Christ Church; they died within five days of each other in January 1898. An earlier building on this site was occupied in 1452 by the Master of Kepier hospital.

Older still is the church of St Mary-the-Less, almost tucked away across the road from no. 4, which is now part of St John's College and for which since 1919 it has been the chapel. Built originally in the 12th century by the mighty Nevilles of Brancepeth Castle, the church was rebuilt in 1846-47 by Pickering who re-used some of the original stone and probably followed the original floor plan. Amongst other monuments in this building is one to a diminutive man who was larger than life in the city's history, Joseph Boruwlaski, referred to even today as 'the Polish dwarf'. Although he was buried in the cathedral, his memorial was erected here because the wording on it was felt to be inappropriate to the great church. Some of what has previously been written about this little man has been inaccurate; he did not ever, for example, live in what is now known as Count's House, a garden house of the 1820s in the style of a Greek Doric temple on the banks of the Wear near Prebends' Bridge. The house he did occupy, not far away, is now long gone. Joseph Boruwlaski was famous primarily for his size; he was just 39 inches tall when fully grown and, although always something of a curiosity, he established himself as a respected member of Durham society. Born near Chaliez in Poland in 1739, he was one of six children born to perfectly normally-proportioned parents. Three of the offspring grew to a normal size while the others remained unusually small. Although Joseph

52. Gateway leading from the college into the bailey.

53. St Mary-the-Less, South Bailey.

was so small, however, his body was perfectly proportioned. The Boruwlaski family had once been wealthy but Joseph's father died when the boy was only nine years old. A friend of the family, Countess Humieski (sometimes Humiecka or Humieska) 'adopted' him and, when he was 15 and not yet three feet tall, took him on a tour of the courts of Europe. He was regarded as something of a sensation and was fêted everywhere he went; he became used to mingling with monarchs and courtiers and was renowned for his tact and courtesy. On one occasion, as he notes in his memoirs, he was presented to the Empress Maria Theresa who sat him on her knee. Noticing that Joseph was gazing at her hand, the Empress thought that he was looking at a fine ring she was wearing. She offered it to him but he explained that it was not the ring but her hand at which he had been gazing; he then asked leave to kiss it. The Empress was so charmed that she removed her ring and tried to fit it onto the little man's finger; it was far too big and just slipped off. She then called over a six-year-old girl who was herself wearing a very attractive ring. Having asked the child for it, she slipped it onto Boruwlaski's finger. He treasured the gift all his life, for the child who had owned the ring was Marie Antoinette, who became the ill-fated wife of Louis XVI of France and was to lose her head before the century was out.

When Boruwlaski was 25, he fell in love with a French actress. His love was unrequited, however, and he returned to Poland and the countess who sheltered him. For almost 15 years he remained with her but then fell in love with a lady called Isalina Barboutan, companion to the countess. When the countess discovered the romance, she sent Isalina back home and locked Boruwlaski in his room for two weeks. On his release he was informed in no uncertain terms that he had but two choices, either to remain with the countess or to leave her house forever. He chose the latter course but was deeply upset at having to leave the lady who had shown him so much kindness. Not having enough money to support his Isalina, Boruwlaski approached the ruler of Poland, who awarded him a pension. Despite this generosity, Boruwlaski was still short of money and decided that, for the first time in his life, he would have to earn a living. His only perceptible skill was as a violinist and he embarked on yet another tour of the European courts looking for a new patron. In 1782 Boruwlaski was presented at the English court and met the Duke of Gloucester who befriended him. Sadly, both the Duke and another new friend died, leaving the Pole again to fend for himself. He determined to make a new start in America but, before he could sail, two ladies gave him enough money to remain in England. Boruwlaski left London and settled, eventually, in Durham, where he shared the home of his great friend Mr. Ebdon and his family in The Grove. He was very popular with cathedral society, several of whose members had special cutlery made for him to use when he dined with them.

Boruwlaski once wrote in an autograph book:

Poland was my cradle,
England is my nest,
Durham is my quiet place
Where my bones shall rest.

That they most certainly did. When he died in September 1837 he was almost 99 years old.

No. 12 South Bailey is well known for two reasons: as the main house for the St Cuthbert's Society and for the incredible late Victorian moulding, a pure flight of fancy, over the main entrance. The property was originally two

54.   The Watergate and City Walls from Prebends' Bridge.

55. Prebends' Bridge from Count's corner.

56. Prebends' Bridge, looking downstream.

57. Durham Cathedral and the old fulling mill.

58. Sir Walter Scott's famous words on Prebends' Bridge.

houses, one 17th-, the other 19th-century. The end of the South Bailey is marked by the Water gate, a plain arch built in 1778 in the old bailey wall by the Rev. Henry Egerton, primarily to allow better access for horse-drawn vehicles to the Baileys from Prebends' Bridge (so-called because only the prebends or canons of the cathedral have the right to drive a vehicle across it). The Water Gate replaced the old medieval gateway. No traveller along the Baileys should stop at the Water Gate; a short descent down an unmade road leads to Prebends' Bridge, from which is to be had one of the finest and best-known views of Durham Cathedral.

Chapter Nine

Silver Street to Aykley Heads

The steep and curving Silver Street, today a pedestrianised shopping thoroughfare, connects Market Place with North Road via Framwellgate Bridge.

59. Silver Street, from *The Graphic*, 1883.

In the environs of the present no. 39 there once stood the home of one of Durham's most famous residents, Sir John Duck, a man who reputedly owed his good luck to a raven. His house was demolished in 1964. John Duck was not a native of Durham but came to the city as a young man. He was probably born at Kilton in what is now the County of Cleveland in 1634; in his will he specifically mentions the poor of that village. Precisely when he came to Durham, or why, is not known, but it was probably as an adolescent as he married his employer's daughter in Durham's St Nicholas' church on 30 July 1655. The young Duck seems to have arrived in Durham without a penny to his name, seeking his fortune and looking for employment as a butcher's apprentice.

Since he was not a member of the Butchers' Guild, however, he found that gaining employment was no easy matter. After several fruitless attempts to contact someone who would give him the opportunity to demonstrate his worth, he met a butcher called John Heslop who, contrary to guild practice, accepted him as his apprentice.

The wedding of Ann Heslop and John Duck was performed in the presence of the Mayor of Durham, John Airson, but the future for the young couple was not to be as rosy as it may have seemed. John Heslop had obviously offended other guild members by employing Duck, as demonstrated by this record in the books of the Incorporated Company of Butchers of the City of Durham:

Memorandum. That on Tuesday, 12th January, 1656, being one of the quarter meetinge dayes, Robert Blunt and Clement Ladler, Wardens of this Company of Butchers gave John Heslopp warning that from henceforth hee forebeare to sett John Duck on work in the trade of a butcher upon payne for every default 39s. 11d.

60.   Timber-framed building in Silver Street.

Heslop could only dismiss his apprentice. Rather than embarrass his father-in-law through further argument with the guild, John Duck decided that his future lay elsewhere and made plans to leave Durham. Fate then intervened, it seems, in a most remarkable way.

The story is told that Duck was on the banks of the River Wear, walking towards Framwellgate Bridge to make his way out of the city, when he observed a raven flying above him with something shiny in its beak. As he walked the bird followed him and, when he was crossing the bridge, it swooped low and released the gold crown coin it had been carrying. He watched the bird fly away and then bent down to retrieve the money. As he was examining it, a farmer berating the two cows he was attempting to drive approached Duck across the bridge. Asking what the problem was, Duck learned that the man had been having trouble with the animals all day. They struck a bargain, and he exchanged his coin for the two troublesome creatures which he soon sold, at a profit, in the market-place. Having an eye to the main chance and giving up all thought of starting life anew elsewhere, John Duck used that profit to continue dealing in cattle. Despite not having completed his apprenticeship and facing possible opposition from the guild, he also began to trade as a butcher. He gradually made a great deal of money and, as is often the way, became a highly-respected citizen. In 1680 John Duck was not only installed as Mayor of the City of Durham but was given the freedom of the Butchers' Company: 'John Duck Esq. Maior of the Cittie of Durham is admitted with the consent of the Company a freeman of the Fraternity of Butchers, and have paid for such his said admission 13s. 4d'.

John Duck used some of his wealth to buy an estate at Haswell. He also became the owner of several coal mines, leasing others from the Church at Durham. He also made money in this new venture, and in 1686 he became a baronet. During the same year he founded a hospital at Lumley and it was at this time that Duck and his wife moved into the Silver Street house. Both Sir John Duck and his wife were buried in Durham's St Margaret's church. He died in 1691 at the age of 59, while Anne died in 1695.

At the head of Silver Street there used to be a hostelry called the *Rose and Crown Hotel* where the people of Durham City presented King Charles I with some silver. The hotel survived into the age of the motor car.

Framwellgate Bridge, overlooked by the impressive western battlements of the castle, was thrown across the River Wear in about 1126 by Bishop Ralph Flambard. Three hundred years later, after it had been badly damaged by floods, its rescue and rebuilding were funded

61. Silver Street from Framwellgate Bridge.

by Bishop Langley along with some monies from the cathedral. There used to be a gatehouse at the east side of the bridge across the roadway, but this was taken down in 1760 when no longer of use; it was, in any case, a hindrance to the free flow of traffic. The bridge was widened in 1856. A delightful record tells how, when work was being carried out on the bridge walls in 1828, a live toad was found inside the masonry, presumed to have been walled up there centuries before. Charming as the story is, it is probable that the creature appeared on the scene from nearby when no workman was looking.

Downriver, the view is primarily of the 1967 Millburngate Bridge, the 1965-69 National Savings Certificate Office in the concrete Millburngate House (which passing motorists assume was not afforded sufficient parking space judging from the permanently congested state of the nearby car park) and the ice-skating rink of the 1940s. To traditionalists the view is not at all inspiring, although it must be admitted that Millburngate Bridge has helped to remove the need for traffic to negotiate

62. Framwellgate Bridge, looking upstream.

Durham city centre, while the National Savings Certificate Office has brought a great deal of employment to the area.

The view upriver is primarily of Prebends' Bridge and the Old Fulling Mill, now the Museum of Archaeology. Opposite, across the river, is the old Corn Mill. While the Corn Mill was certainly in existence before the end of the 12th century, the Fulling Mill dates from the start of the 15th century. It was part of the embryonic weaving trade which was then growing in the city. During the 1950s the Old Fulling Mill was a popular café, after which it was utilised as part of the Department of Archaeology where such eminent academics as Professor Eric Birley and Dr. (later Professor) Rosemary Cramp tutored the new generation of archaeologists, including probably the world's foremost expert on Hadrian's Wall, Dr. David Breeze.

Just across the bridge from Silver Street is the brick-built Millburngate Shopping Complex of 1972-76, designed by the Building Design Partnership. In 1978 it gained several architectural awards. Incorporated into the scheme, almost like part of a backdrop to a Walt Disney cartoon film, is a small, heavily restored but essentially 14th-century, timber-framed house, found on the site as it was being cleared.

The Millburngate shopping complex really marks the Framwellgate Bridge end of North Road, once a major route to the north, formerly known as King Street because it was opened in 1831, the year of William IV's coronation. The contemporary

63.   The old fulling mill and its weir.

64. The railway viaduct, from the cathedral tower.

65. From *The Graphic*, 1883, showing the City of Durham from the railway.

King William IV public house used to occupy a corner site, where the road across Framwellgate Bridge turned right into Framwellgate itself. The Mill Burn still exists but is channelled under North Road before emptying into the Wear. North Road is now almost completely commercial, totally unlike Saddler Street, the Elvets and the Baileys, with not a lot to commend it except a few good shops. One or two buildings are, however, worthy of note. One is the Miners' Hall, built in 1875 on a grand scale but not used for its original purpose by the middle years of the Great War. It is worth seeing for its solid construction and its octagonal, copper-domed clock tower. The other building is the United Methodist (Bethel) chapel dating from 1853. Its architect was R. Robson. In a city dominated by its cathedral and several beautiful churches, this chapel affords an interesting nonconformist architectural comparison. The top of North Road is dominated by the enormous railway viaduct. With 11 arches and standing 100 ft. high, it dates from 1857. One of the best views of the cathedral, indeed of the whole city, is to be had by rail passengers crossing this bridge. The viaduct carries the railway to Durham's station, set high to the north-west of the city and also built in 1857. The first Durham railway station, built by the Durham and Sunderland Railway in 1839, was in the nearby village of Shincliffe. It operated until 1893, in which year Elvet station opened, at the head of Old Elvet, and was in use until 1931. The Magistrates' courts were built on the site when it was demolished in 1963. In 1844 a station designed by G. T. Andrews was opened in Gilesgate, a spur connecting that point with the London to Newcastle line at Belmont Junction. In 1857 this became a goods-only station, eventually closing in 1966.

Set in an elevated position below the station, and a familiar sight to rail passengers and others near this end of North Road is the large and elegant Roman Catholic church of Our Lady of Mercy and St Godric in Castle Chare. It was built in 1864 by E. W. Pugin, primarily to offer a place of worship for the large number of Irish workers who came to the area during the 19th century. The west tower was added in 1909.

One route to County Durham's administrative heart, County Hall at Aykley Heads, is via Framwellgate Bridge and along New Millburngate. Up on the left is the Castle Chare Arts Centre, the building itself dating from about 1741. It was in turn an inn and a convent before becoming an arts centre, but its real fame rests on some beautiful plaster work for which, if for no other reason, the centre should be visited.

Framwellgate rises up a hill towards the north-west, passing Sidegate, or Sidgate, which leads to Crook Hall, a property which has links with the Battle of Neville's Cross. The manor house here seems to have started life in the 14th century, although some architectural historians believe it to have been begun in about 1286. It is probable that the builder was one Peter del Croke, hence Croke Hall. The Neville's Cross connection is that Joan del Croke married John de Copeland, the man who at that battle took prisoner the Scottish King David. From the end of the 14th century until 1667 the property was owned by the Billingham family, one of whom was to have a serious argument with the citizens of Durham. It was in the 15th century that the philanthropic Thomas Billingham allowed water from the Fram Well, which he owned, to be piped into Durham Market Place, and so it flowed for almost two centuries. In 1636 the supply suddenly dried up; on investigation it was found that

66.   The famous view from Durham station.

Cuthbert Billingham, the owner of Crook Hall, had diverted the supply away from
the city to power his mills. It transpired that an annual rent of some 13d. for the
water had apparently not been paid and a lengthy legal battle ensued. A year later,
however, the situation was resolved and the water supply resumed. Subsequent
owners of Crook Hall were the Mickletons and the Hoppers, while a famous tenant
was the 19th-century Durham historian, James Raine. A 17th-century extension links
the old property to an 18th-century brick house of three storeys.

    Beyond the railway bridge, to the north of the road, is the Durham Light Infantry
Museum and Arts Centre. Built here at Aykley Heads between 1964-68 by Tarren and
Caller, it was once described as 'a glass box' but stages some superb exhibitions and
houses a permanent collection outlining the history of the county's own regiment.
The Durham Light Infantry, raised in 1758 and existing until 1968, marched at the
rate of 160 paces per minute. It was a famous regiment with many battle honours.
Some of its flags are to be seen in the D.L.I. chapel in the cathedral.

    The dominant building in this area, a short distance further along the road, is
Durham's County Hall, started in 1960 and completed some three years later at a
cost of £2½ million. The architects were, first, G. R. Clayton the County Architect,
and then the next man to occupy that post, G. W. Gelson. Most of the brick but faced
building rises to six storeys. Housed within County Hall is the County Record Office,

67. Emblem of the Durham Light Infantry.

with its helpful staff. The building replaced the Old Shire Hall, now Durham University's administrative offices, in Old Elvet. Arguably the greatest treasure in County Hall is a wonderful, expansive and colourful mural by Spennymoor pit-man artist Norman Cornish, whose work is now highly prized worldwide; it depicts what was once Durham's busiest event, the Miners' Gala, colliery banners, beer bottles, brass bands and all. Cornish has painted himself into the work sitting, as a small boy, on his father's shoulders.

On the other side of the road leading to Framwellgate Moor is Dryburn Hospital, begun during the Second World War in the grounds of what was Dryburn Hall, subsequently Dryburn House, built in 1824 for William Lloyd Wharton, Sheriff of Durham.

Beyond Bethel chapel is a roundabout, over which North Road continues past the County Hospital, opened in 1853, past Wharton Park with its obelisk, erected in 1850 at a point 1,200 yards north of the University Observatory, to the road's junction with Framwellgate and the church of St Cuthbert. Its architect was E. R. Robson; the church was built between 1858 and 1863. Wharton Park itself was given to the citizens of Durham in 1915 by W. L. Wharton's daughter, Mrs. Darwin.

Chapter Ten

Elvet Bridge, the Elvets and Church Street

Fleshergate, with Saddler Street, is the main road from the Market Place to the cathedral and castle but a turn to the left at the Magdalen Steps leads to Elvet Bridge which carries the pedestrianised road across the river to the Elvets.

The bridge was built by Bishop Hugh Pudsey in about 1160, had further work carried out on it in 1228 and was further and more extensively repaired by Bishop Fox in 1495. Of the original 14 arches recorded by the historian Leland only 10 now remain and two of these are obscured by subsequent buildings. There used to be a chapel at each end of the bridge: that to the east, on the site of the Dutch-gabled building, was dedicated to St Andrew and built in the 13th century, while that on the west end was dedicated to St James. It was replaced by part of the House of Correction in 1632. Some of this latter establishment can still be clearly seen, bars and all, at the bottom of the steps leading from the bridge down to the river. Nearby is Brown's boathouse, where boats may be rented by those wishing to take to the water. Brown's is also famous for constructing racing fours and eights, as seen at Henley or at Durham's own and much older regatta. Much of Elvet Bridge was destroyed during the great and infamous flood of 1771. Between 1804-5 the width of the old bridge was doubled.

The House of Correction, under the bridge, was the last home of a character once as famous throughout the land as Robin Hood is today. He was Jamie Allan, a celebrated Northumbrian piper and sometime villain. It is said that his is one of the ghosts which haunts Durham, the strains of his pipes still being heard around Elvet Bridge. Jamie Allan, sometimes known as Jemmy or Jimmy, was a gypsy born in about 1734 near Rothbury in Northumberland. His story is a remarkable one. John Sykes reports his death:

13th November, 1810. Died in the House of Correction at Durham, where he had been confined upwards of seven years, under sentence of transportation for life, James Allan, a character well-known in most parts of the United Kingdom, particularly in Northumberland, where he was known by the name of Jemmy, the duke's piper, and was in early life a great proficient on the pipes. He was capitally convicted of horse-stealing, at the assizes held in Durham, in 1803, and received sentence of death, but was afterwards pardoned on condition of transportation for life; but on account of his age and infirmities, his sentence could not be carried into execution. He had nearly completed his 77th year, and, for the greatest part of his confinement, was afflicted with a complication of disorders. Had the chequered life of this notorious character been prolonged a little, he would have regained his liberty, as the first signature of the Prince Regent, officially addressed to the city of Durham, was a free pardon for Allan; but death had removed him beyond the reach of royal clemency.

68. Elvet Bridge from the towpath.

69. Approach to Elvet Bridge from Saddler Street.

70. Gateway to the old House of Correction below Elvet Bridge.

71. Interior of the old House of Correction, below Elvet Bridge.

72.   Portrait of Jamie Allan, the piper.

Many adventures are ascribed to Allan but few can be verified and, like Robin Hood, he is always regarded as a romantic figure despite his obvious faults.

Allan is said to have played his pipes before royalty, was married at least three times, once bigamously, and frequently enlisted in and deserted from the army. There is no apparent explanation of why the Prince Regent was so ready to pardon him. James Allan was youngest-but-one of a family of six. Taking up the pipes at the age of 14, he learned quickly from his father. It is noted that as a piper he possessed an accurate ear, a refined taste and great sensibility to the beauties of harmony. He was remarkably adroit at learning a new tune and was admired for the exquisite expression of feeling and simplicity which distinguished his performances. His biographer in 1828 records that he 'could play on the highland bagpipe but he excelled most on the sweet small pipes. He also played well on the Northumberland raising or gathering pipes, called the 'great pipes' to distinguish them from the small ones; and could perform very well on the Union pipes'. Allan was summoned to play to the Countess of Northumberland and was, according to some sources, made her piper. She gave him a 'pair of small pipes she had procured from Edinburgh, handsomely-made of ivory and decorated with silver chains' when he left her service. He was given a second set of pipes by the next Duchess of Northumberland.

Allan was interred in St Nicholas' churchyard, Durham, although he had asked to be buried at Rothbury. His pipes he left to 'two gentlemen of North Shields', the port where he spent his winters when he was a free man. A few verses were written about Jamie Allan soon after his death:

All ye whom Music's charms inspire
Who skilful minstrels do admire.
All ye whom bagpipe lilts can fire
'Tween Wear and Tweed,
Come, strike with me, the mournful lyre,
For ALLAN's dead.

No more where Coquet's stream doth glide
Shall we view JEMMY in his pride,
With bagpipe buckled to his side,
And nymphs and swains
In groups collect, at even-tide,
To hear his strains.

When elbow moved, and bellows blew,
On green or floor the dancers flew,
In many turns ran through and through
With cap'ring canter,
And aye their nimble feet beat true
To his sweet chanter.

Across Elvet Bridge are the two Elvets, Old and New. Elvet is derived from the Saxon *aelfet ee*, meaning swan island. Today New Elvet leads down to New Elvet Bridge, a new crossing slightly upstream from Elvet Bridge. The *Waterloo Hotel* was demolished in 1971 to create access to it.

Old Elvet was once considered to be among the finest streets in the whole county but is felt to have been spoiled by the building of the Shire Hall and the Methodist church between 1895 and 1903. Nevertheless, it is still a wide and attractive thorough-fare with some beautiful architecture. First to be encountered across Elvet Bridge is the fine *Royal County Hotel*, a hostelry with a fascinating history. The present luxurious establishment is an amalgam of several buildings of varying dates and the property seen today was formerly 57-60 Old Elvet along with the now-vanished Chapel Passage. The famous balcony across the central frontage of the hotel was created in two parts, the stone balustrade early in the 19th century, the ironwork in the late 19th century. For a short time in the late 18th century, part of the building was used as a boarding school. The original properties on this site, now much changed, date from *c*.1630. One was the home of Lady Mary Radcliffe, a member of the famous Roman Catholic Derwentwater family of Dilston Castle. Her half-sister was Lady Mary Tudor, natural daughter to King Charles II. Her nephews, James and Charles Radcliffe, were great supporters of the Jacobite cause, James involving himself in the rebellion of 1715, Charles in that of 1745. Mention having just been made of Jamie Allan, the Northumbrian piper, it is interesting to note that Charles Radcliffe is reputed to have bidden farewell to the north country on the spot now occupied by the *Cock o' the North Hotel* on the A167 road, and that *Derwentwater's Farewell* is still a popular tune with Northumbrian pipers.

Another of the houses was occupied by Elizabeth Bowes, aunt to the Earl of Strath-more's wife, Mary Eleanor Bowes. It was she who inherited the vast properties of the

COUNTY HOTEL,

DURHAM,

LATE

WARD'S WATERLOO.

FAMILY, COMMERCIAL,

AND

POSTING HOUSE,

THOMAS TURNER,

PROPRIETOR,

(Late of the King's Head, Darlington).

An OMNIBUS to and from the Station.

CABS ON HIRE.

WINES & SPIRITS

Of the best Quality, from a quarter of a Pint upwards.

73. 19th-century advertisement for the *County Hotel*.

Bowes family, but her father's will insisted that her husband had to take her family name. So it was that John Lyon, Earl of Strathmore, took the name of Bowes, even though an Act of Parliament was required to enable this to happen. Thus was established the link with the property to Lady Elizabeth Bowes Lyon, a member of that family and queen to King George VI. Elizabeth Bowes owned the house from 1758; after her death, it passed to the Earl of Strathmore and stayed in that family until the 19th century. Thereafter it was for a time the *Dunelm Hotel*. One of the peculiarities of this site is that for a long time there were two neighbouring hostelries which were both known as the *Waterloo*, named after the great British victory of 1815. The now-demolished *Waterloo Hotel*, formerly 61 Old Elvet, appears to have been known in its earliest days as the *Green Dragon Inn*. It is difficult to ascertain when either property first became a hostelry although it is certain that the present *Royal County* was known as the *Waterloo Hotel* in 1820, for in that year the owner, William

Ward, was advertising his premises in a local gazetteer. Presumably the name *Waterloo* was taken soon after the battle, such was national pride in the victory. By 1827, Ward's hotel was advertised as the *Waterloo Hotel and Posting House*. In 1834, the property had passed to Elizabeth Ward and was again known simply as the *Waterloo Hotel*. By 1846, no. 61 was also advertising itself as the *Waterloo Hotel*, run by John Thwaites, victualler; in 1827, he had run the *Queen's Head Inn and Posting House* in the North Bailey, which inn he administered until moving to the *Waterloo*. On old maps the two Old Elvet properties are distinctly shown as Ward's *Waterloo Hotel* and Thwaites' *Waterloo Hotel*. Elizabeth Ward was succeeded by the Ward brothers in 1850, but in 1851 the place was run by W. Thomas Ward. Strangely enough, in 1850 both properties were called the *Waterloo Hotel and Commercial Inn* but in 1864 there was a change. The Thwaites' property, no. 61, became the *Waterloo Inn* while no. 60 passed from the ownership of the Wards to one Thomas Turner, formerly an hotelier in Darlington, and changed its name to the *County Hotel*. In 1866 the Thwaites gave up the *Waterloo* which was taken over by A. Millar, while the *County* passed into the hands of Mrs. Turner. Thereafter, while the *Waterloo Hotel* changed hands fairly frequently, the *County*, owned by Mrs. Turner until 1871, was then run by Mrs. White until well into the 1880s. Sometime before 1900, after a visit by Albert, Prince of Wales (to become King Edward VII in 1901), the *County* became the *Royal County Hotel* and was administered by a progression of manageresses. How the post office managed to discern which *Waterloo* was which in the early days of the hotels will never be known.

Even before the *Royal County* was an hotel it had at least two famous visitors. Oliver Cromwell is said to have stayed in one of the houses in 1650 on his journey to the Battle of Dunbar and King Charles I, according to local tradition, hid somewhere on the premises before his arrest and execution.

The amalgamation of the separate buildings into a single entity has been skilfully achieved and much of Durham's 'old world charm' is encapsulated here. Something which is not 'of Durham' is the hotel's wonderful black staircase, dating originally from *c.*1660; it was brought and re-erected here from Loch Leven Castle in Scotland. Today an archway marks the way from Old Elvet into the hotel car park. In the past, this site was occupied by a brewery, farriers and livery stables. In 1867, at 57 Old Elvet, John Wilkie advertised his services as an omnibus driver. By 1874, at the same address and at Elvet Waterside, William Wilkie, presumably a relative, was proprietor of the *County Hotel* livery stables and in 1877, still at 57 Old Elvet, a William Wilkie was in business as a cab proprietor. The former Chapel Passage, no longer there, used to cross what is now the car park and led to the Methodist chapel, opened in 1808 and demolished in 1968. Beside it was a three-storey house for the preacher. This was the second Methodist chapel in the city, an earlier one having existed in Court Lane, probably simply a converted dwelling house.

Many people know the *Royal County Hotel*'s famous balcony, on which prominent Labour Party and mineworkers' leaders have stood over the years to watch the parade of bands and lodge banners of the Durham coal mines on Gala Day, better known locally as Durham Big Meeting. Today the event is but a shadow of its former self, coal mines being now almost non-existent in the county, but for decades it was the focal point, on the third Saturday in July, for every miner and his family. The

74. Late Victorian cricket match on the old racecourse.

present Miners' Hall, successor to that in North Road, is in Redhills Lane. Its architect
from 1913-15, H. T. Gradon, and its finest feature, the immense council chamber. It
may seem today something of an anachronism, but in its day it was a crucial seat of
power. Today the miners and associated trade unions meet on Smiddyhaughs, the
fields which were the city's racecourse from 1733-1887, but this was not always the
ultimate venue. Many of the miners and their families paraded to Palace Green and a
service in the cathedral. The first Durham Miners' Gala was held not on the racecourse but in Wharton Park on 2 August 1871, just two years after the Durham
Miners' Association was founded. At its height, the event was the largest annual
demonstration by the working classes anywhere in the country; just before the First
World War the crowds were often in excess of 100,000 people. In 1882 a Russian
prince, Propotkin, addressed the assembled throng. At times even the colliery

75.   A rather romantic view of a Durham miner at home, from the *London Illustrated News*.

owners were allowed to take part in the proceedings. There were no meetings during the First World War but in 1925, the year before the General Strike, some of the Durham miners marked their gala by throwing the Dean of Durham into the River

Wear; what actually happened was that they mistook him for the Bishop of Durham who had expressed the view that miners did not deserve an increase in pay. They carried banners proclaiming 'To Hell with Bishops and Deans. We demand a living wage'. After the Second World War, during which the Gala was again suspended, so many people began to attend the gathering that the racecourse was equipped with two platforms for speakers. The great names of the Labour party appeared on these stages and on the *Royal County Hotel*'s balcony: Clement Attlee, Stafford Cripps, Herbert Morrison, Ernest Bevin, Aneurin Bevan, Harold Wilson, Michael Foot and Tony Benn all came in recognition of the importance of the event to the Labour Movement. The event now relies on the support of more than just miners and their families for its survival but that survival, in one form or another, does seem assured.

Behind the *Royal County Hotel* is Elvet Waterside, now very much a backwater, and the site of the new, and tasteful, hotel extension and some private houses. Before the building of the New Elvet Bridge, the Elvets were directly linked with Claypath and Gilesgate by a succession of Baths Bridges. The baths themselves, designed by John Augustus Cory, were built in 1855. The first of the footbridges, of wood in this instance, was also erected in 1855 and was replaced by an iron one in 1898. The present footbridge was opened in 1962. Most of the buildings in Old Elvet date from the 17th to the 19th century. It is worth noting how many of the properties still have boot-scrapers at their doors.

Beyond the *Royal County Hotel* car park archway is 55-53 Old Elvet, now a single building, which excites considerable interest because of its beautiful classical architecture and for the two small cannon which stand in front of it. These are actually carronades, dating from the very early 19th century and manufactured in Scotland at the Carronbridge Iron Foundry. They were brought here from Tynemouth in the 1950s. Across the road, set back on the south side, is the stone-built Elvet Methodist church of 1906, the first of two buildings considered by many to have spoiled the lines of Old Elvet. Near this is the essentially redbrick Old Shire Hall, once called a 'grotesque monstrosity', built between 1895-8 and enlarged in 1905. The original architects were Harry Barnes and Frederick Coates, both local men, the former becoming a Member of Parliament. The builder was Rankin of Sunderland. The building has much to recommend it. Its copper-coloured dome is something of a landmark; its entrance hall is tiled to a degree which fascinates the visitor; and the council chamber is acoustically superb. There is a great deal of Weardale marble in its make-up along with stained glass from Glasgow and woodwork from Newcastle. Much as the building has often been criticised, it is a superb piece of architecture. To visit it is to step back in time, to savour Victoriana at its most welcoming. Since 1963, when Durham County Council moved its headquarters to Aykley Heads, the Old Shire Hall has been the administrative centre of Durham University. Many of the properties in Old Elvet are now owned by the university and are, in fact, university departments.

No. 46 Old Elvet was at one time the office of the architect Ignatius Bonomi, while no. 34 was once occupied by a relative by marriage of Lord Byron and, later, by the Victorian hymn writer John Bacchus Dykes, precentor of the cathedral and best remembered today for his hymn *Eternal Father, strong to save*. He resigned as precentor

76.   Baths footbridge, from the racecourse.

77.   Pleasure cruiser on the Wear above Baths footbridge.

78.   Old Shire Hall, Old Elvet.

to become vicar of nearby St Oswald's church from 1862-74. He lies buried in the churchyard extension. No. 32 Old Elvet still retains its small ballroom. On the north side of Old Elvet, where the street opens into a wider area with a green, is the Masonic Hall of 1869, designed by a local architect called Thomas Ebdy. Its elaborate style marks it as something of an oddity in this essentially simple street. The site of the former Elvet railway station is now occupied by the brick Magistrates Courts, one of a suite of judicial buildings in this part of Durham.

Across the road from the Magistrates Courts is the new part of Durham Prison, while a short way across the green, at the end of Court Lane, are the original Durham Prison and the Old Assize Courts or Crown Courts. Much controversy surrounded the building of these. Begun in 1809, their first architect, Francis Sandys, was dismissed; he was followed by George Moneypenny and then by Ignatius Bonomi, who completed the project to his own plan. In 1870 the inside of the building was completely redesigned. Bonomi also completed the gaol between 1815-19; it was enlarged in 1850. That part of Bonomi's building originally used to house female prisoners later became Durham prison's famous E-Wing.

One of the strangest facts about Old Elvet and its green is that it was, until the middle of this century, the venue for a horse fair, moved here from the Market Place. It is difficult now to imagine men and women trotting horses up and down this famous street to demonstrate that all was well with the animals they were attempting to sell, but they did so until the 1950s.

Across from the Courts is another of Ignatius Bonomi's buildings, St Cuthbert's Roman Catholic church of 1827. The tower was not added until 1869.

79.   Dunelm House, New Elvet, from below Kingsgate Bridge.

Court Lane, or Ratenraw as it used to be known, links Old Elvet with New Elvet, to some a disappointing thoroughfare now with much new building. The only building in the street with anything to commend it is the former coaching inn the *Three Tuns Hotel*. Across the road from the *Three Tuns* are the university's Elvet Riverside Buildings of 1966 and 1975, functional but basically unattractive. Near them is a facility which must have excited more discussion and controversy than any other in Durham; this is Dunelm House, another university property, designed by William Powers as a series of stacked grey concrete boxes supported, it appears, by kerb stones, chipping at the edges. From New Elvet it is unpleasant; from the river and Kingsgate Bridge it is arguably worse. It has won both Civic Trust and R.I.B.A. awards.

At Dunelm House the road forks, that to the right becoming Church Street, while to the left is Hallgarth Street. A lane off Hallgarth Street leads to a mid-15th-century tithe barn, once the property of the monks but now used as a club. Hallgarth Street has long been an unfashionable address, many of its 18th-and 19th-century brick terraced houses being let to students, but genuine interest is at last being taken in

80. St Oswald's church, New Elvet.

the street's unassuming charm. Hallgarth Street now ends at a roundabout; a left turn leads along Whinney Hill and back to Old Elvet; the road straight ahead leads to the university's sports facility at Maiden Castle, to Houghall College, Shincliffe village and the east; to the right is Stockton Road with its new university library and science block, standing where the miners of Elvet Pit once brought coals to the surface. Across the road from the university library are several attractive terraces of mainly Victorian houses; one of these, Gladstone Villas, carries a plaque with the bust of the eminent Victorian statesman after whom the houses are named.

Church Street is the setting for the beautiful St Oswald's church, dedicated to the Christian Northumbrian monarch who died in 642 and whose skull is interred in Cuthbert's tomb. The church stands high above the river gorge and faces the cathedral. The date of the foundation of this church is difficult to establish, the oldest parts of the present building being late 12th-century. By 1834 land subsidence and general neglect of the site necessitated the first of several renovations. This was undertaken by Ignatius Bonomi. Further work was carried out 30 years later, when a number of medieval grave covers were used to repair the tower stairs and Hodgson Fowler added the vestry to the chancel. Several pieces of Anglo-Saxon stonework have been found on this site, fuelling the theory that there was an earlier church here, but after the great and tragic fire in 1984 there was a chance for archaeologists to discover what type of church had previously occupied this site. Stonework dating from before the Norman Conquest has been found here; in 762, Peohtwine was consecrated Bishop of Galloway somewhere in Elvet; 15th-and 16th-century maps of the area appear to show that the church had a circular, Saxon-type graveyard. What the archaeologists found was that there had been an earlier church on the site with a typically Saxon apsidal or semicircular east end. Included in the church's several memorials are those to Edward Walter Clervaux Chaytor, Aide-de Camp to King George V, and to William Green, for 44 years honorary surgeon to the Durham Infirmary. The fire of 1984, started by an arsonist, began in the organ chamber and did considerable damage to the chancel and its roof, but spared most of the 14th-century pews. A great deal of thought was given to the matter of replacing the organ; the eventual decision was that the new instrument, built by Peter Collins, should be situated at the west end of the church. Despite the fact that a busy road runs right past it, the churchyard of St Oswald's is one of the most peaceful places in the city.

Near the church are Anchorage Terrace, originally built as single-storey cottages for the miners of Elvet Pit, and Anchorage House, nothing to do with safe havens but recording instead the story that on or near their site in the Middle Ages was a hermit's cell. A cotton factory existed in Church Street from 1796-1804, in which year it was destroyed by fire.

Chapter Eleven

Claypath and Gilesgate

Claypath is the eastern exit from the Market Place. Its continuation is Gilesgate, once called Gillygate, the old road to Sunderland. Modern management schemes have produced new roads which have eased the city's former traffic problems but have cut into both Claypath and Gilesgate, radically altering their former character. Claypath is now a shadow of its former self, seeming to be cut off from the rest of Durham and little visited by those not having particular business there. Guarding this exit from the Market Place was the Clayport or Claypath Gate. It was gone by Hutchinson's time; the 1823 edition of his *History and Antiquities of the County Palatine of Durham* records that it was:

> a weak edifice, nearly similar to that which lately stood in the South-Bailey, called the Water-gate, having no machiolation, and only the appearance of a single pair of gates, built with irregular stones and much mortar; the present remains of the city wall shew it was of similar construction, remarked by Leland to be of mean masonry: This gate had a foot passage at the east side. Why this gateway appeared so weak, may be owing to the out-works being completely defaced; and here, in particular, if there was a water-sluice, with a draw-bridge, as we presume there was, less strength was required in the gateway.

81. Quaker meeting house, Claypath.

Claypath itself is quite a steep thoroughfare with mainly Georgian and Victorian architecture, little of it remarkable. On its south side are the old Quaker burial ground and the site, now occupied by modern housing, of the former Bluecoat School. There is a little more new building in the immediate area. Further up the bank, on the same side, is a very attractive street called Leazes Place; although built in the 1840s it is essentially late Georgian in design and is one of the most pleasant parts of Durham. Leazes House, built at about the same time for John Henderson, the carpet manufacturer, was subsequently occupied by Durham High School until 1968, at which time the pupils moved to the new purpose-built establishment near the crematorium.

On the north side of Claypath, leaving the Market Place, are a few shops and the United Reformed church, built in 1885 to H. T. Gradon's design. Completely hidden by it is the brick-built and very plain chapel of 1751; it was successively Presbyterian, Independent and then Congregational. The old general post office marks the beginning of Providence Row, a very steep descent to the River Wear and the area known as the Sands. This is also a route to the ice-skating rink, to the former and world-famous Durham Carpet Factory of Hugh Mackay and Co., and to what remains of the medieval Kepier Hospital. On Providence Row is the school which used to be the old Durham Girls' Grammar School, originally of 1913 but with extensions of 1938 and 1963.

Along the riverbank to the east is the farm which contains what is left of Kepier Hospital. This dates originally from 1112 when it was founded, as St Giles' Hospital in Gilesgate, by Bishop Ralph Flambard; its chapel was St Giles' church. It was Bishop Pudsey who moved it to the riverside late in the 12th century. Its staff, a master and 13 brothers, were charged with the duty of helping the poor of the area, although they did on several occasions entertain royalty here too. What is left to be seen today is the 14th-century gateway, with some building of about the same date in the adjoining farm.

A left turn at the bottom of Providence Row leads to the site of the medieval Bishop's Mill and to what used to be the Mackay Carpet Factory, a concern which has now moved to the city's outskirts. Many people are proud to own a Durham carpet but few may know much, if anything, of the firm's history. Cloth was certainly woven in Durham as early as 1243 and, in the years that followed, the Guild of Weavers was active in many ways, not least in attempting on several occasions to establish training facilities for young men, and eventually for young girls, to learn the trade. Not all of these ventures were successful; in fact some were abject failures, with evidence that the teachers were defrauding those who had provided their funds. By 1737, however, John Starforth, 'weaver and manufacturer', was awarded a loan of £392 14s. 0d. 'to develop woollen manufacture in Durham City'. By 1774, Starforth was employing 'some hundreds of persons'. During the 1790s he had 700 weavers and was concentrating his efforts on woollen and carpet cloth. By 1801 Starforth's woollen and carpet factory was easily the largest industry in the city: he employed more than 800 workers, over one tenth of the population. Then, in 1805, the business went bankrupt. Several abortive efforts were made to restart weaving in the city and in 1814 one Gilbert Henderson was loaned some £400 to fund his attempt.

Henderson was of Scottish descent and had been employed in the Starforth company; it was he who wound up the company after its failure. By the age of 26, and after a serious illness, he became an invalid, able to move at first only in a wheelchair and then on sticks. He lived in the village of Kirk Merrington, near Spennymoor, where he befriended the local weavers and learned all aspects of their craft. In 1810 he opened a factory in the village to weave carpets; within three years he was employing 60 people in the village. Taking 30 of these employees with him, he

82.   An early-19th century view of the City of Durham.

transferred production at the end of 1813 to Durham City where there already existed the carpet factory of Gainforth and Blackett. His business flourished, despite the workers being involved in a long strike in 1819. In order to produce Brussels carpets he brought what were known as Brussels looms to the city, all but smuggled out of Kidderminster. In 1824 there was a disastrous fire at the factory and in the same year, at the age of 42, Gilbert Henderson died. His wife Ann took over the running of the business, while his elder son John, then aged 17, was still serving his time in the factory learning every aspect of carpet production. In 1828 John Henderson began to run the factory. The business continued to expand and prosper, and in 1835 his brother, William, joined him. John Henderson was elected Liberal Member of Parliament for Durham while William, a Conservative, became Mayor of Durham in 1849 and is remembered for his part in the building of the new Town Hall.

In 1854 steam power was introduced to work the looms alongside the existing handlooms. By exhibiting its wares at the Great Exhibition of 1851 the company found even wider fame. Eventually both John and William withdrew from active management of the firm. John's sons attempted to take up the reins, Arthur Henderson proving himself the most interested and competent. The Henderson Carpet Factory continued in production until 1903 when it was sold to Crossley's. Almost the entire workforce was made redundant.

In 1861, at the age of 12, a boy called Hugh Mackay had begun to work for Henderson's in the weaving shed. By 1880 he was works manager. When Henderson's sold out to Crossley's, Hugh Mackay leased some buildings and machinery not sold to them in order to begin carpet manufacture in his own right. As employees he took on men and women who had worked for Hendersons. His son Laurence came to work for him and started on the factory floor, learning all about the business. It was not long before the 16 looms originally leased from Henderson's were unable to keep up with demand; they were not, in any case, really suitable for the carpet types being produced. Before 1914, Mackay's were producing some of the highest-quality carpets in Britain, one with a pile three-quarters of an inch deep. On Hugh Mackay's death in 1924, his son Laurence took over the business, known since 1921 as Hugh

83.   Remains of the 15th-century chapel of St Mary Madgalene, Gilesgate.

Mackay & Co. Ltd. By 1929, 125 people were employed by the company. In the 1950s John Mackay joined his father as Joint Managing Director; Laurence Mackay died in 1966. Mackays have undertaken dozens of special commissions, one of the most interesting being at the Meeting House in Philadelphia in the U.S.A. Having been provided with little more than a scrap of the carpet which was in use there at the time of the signing of the Declaration of Independence in 1777, Mackay's reproduced that original carpet, perfect in colour and design.

In 1969 a terrible fire, started by an arsonist, severely damaged the factory. In 1980 the company's shareholders agreed that the business should be moved to land bought in 1957 by Laurence Mackay at Dragonville, just over a mile outside Durham City. There it still flourishes today and Durham carpets continue to be among the finest in the world.

Claypath is today essentially separated from Gilesgate by the new road leading to the motorway and Sunderland. Most of today's visitors to Durham never see Gilesgate's ancient streets. On the Claypath side of the new thoroughfare are the ruins of the chapel of St Mary Magdalene, built in 1451 as the chapel for a hospital to care for the old, poor people of the district. The church of St Giles is set back from Gilesgate and has wonderful views well across the river to the cathedral and beyond. Part of the church is the original building, consecrated in 1112 as the chapel of Bishop Ralph Flambard's Hospital of St Giles, established to offer hospitality to pilgrims visiting St Cuthbert's shrine. Gilesgate, with its long village green, has a wealth of buildings in all sorts of styles, dating from the 17th to the 20th century. Energy expended on a walk up and down Gilesgate is amply repaid.

Chapter Twelve

Quarryheads Lane to Pimlico

While the city is rightly famous for its cathedral and castle, there are some who know it for Durham School, a public school of no mean standing and the oldest in the whole county, or for a firm of organ-builders whose work is known across the world.

The *New Inn*, opposite the university science block, is the start of a beautiful walk, missed by many since it is away from the 'tourist honeypot' of the city centre. The walk, in an easterly direction, leads along Quarryheads Lane, past St Mary's College and Bow Preparatory School (the latter established in 1885) to the roundabout at the foot of Potters Bank. Beyond that roundabout the pedestrian can take a footpath to the right, past the lodge and on to Prebends' Bridge, or carry straight on to Durham School.

This is probably one of the oldest educational establishments in Britain, although it is not on its original site. The school could well have existed before William conquered England; it is well known that the abbey had an almonry school immediately outside the gates of the college, but there was an even earlier school than that provided by the monks, established by the bishop himself, possibly on Lindisfarne. Some authorities have suggested that this school was reinstated in Durham as soon as the saint's bones were lodged there in 995. The history of the establishment is almost impossible to trace before the episcopacy of Bishop Thomas Langley (1406-37). It was he who built new premises for it and for the Novices' School on Palace Green, linking the two foundations. The new school had two masters, the senior of whom taught the essentials of Latin, while his junior imparted instruction in the arts of music and singing. Some of the less wealthy scholars attended the school free of charge, while richer parents were charged a fee for their sons' education. With the Reformation royalty took a hand in the school's destiny, King Henry VIII refounding it and establishing the new dean and chapter as its guiding force. The six or so King's Scholarships awarded each year owe their origin to this time. The school was still divided into grammar and song schools with 28 pupils in all, 10 in the song or preparatory school, 18 in the grammar school; these latter were what are recognised today as the King's Scholars. At the grammar school the boys were expected to speak only Latin, and Greek was also studied. They had to attend from 7 a.m. until 5 p.m. with a two-hour break for lunch. It seems that even during their holidays the boys had to attend school twice each day.

In 1844 the school moved to its present Quarryheads Lane site, adapted by Anthony Salvin from an existing house and added to in 1853 and 1862. A number of further additions have been undertaken between 1876 and the present day, including the chapel, which was erected as a war memorial in 1924-26. Durham School can boast many famous old boys; educated here were John Balliol, a lad destined to become King of Scotland, and Robert Smith Surtees of Hamsterley, creator of that

84. South Street.

eternal huntsman, Jorrocks. Another who learned his grammar here was the great Viscount Hardinge, who fought alongside the Duke of Wellington during the Peninsula War. Brought up largely in the Weardale town of Stanhope, he went on to a magnificent career; after becoming Secretary of State for War he was made Governor-General of India and Commander-in-Chief of the British Army, as well as being created Field-Marshal. Durham School today continues the proud traditions and high standards for which it is so rightly famous.

A twisting road winds from Durham School to Crossgate. At the crossroads a left turn leads to Neville's Cross, a right on to Crossgate, while the road ahead takes us to the top of North Road. It is this road which leads to a left turn into Hawthorn Terrace, home for more than a century to a company of real craftsmen, one of the most famous organ-builders in Britain: Harrison and Harrison.

The company was founded by Thomas Harrison who was already an experienced organ-builder by the time he started his own firm in Rochdale, aged just 22, in 1861. His work, of the highest quality from the very start, soon commended him to the world of music. Among his early advocates was the clergyman John Bacchus Dykes of Durham who was instrumental in persuading him and his brother James to transfer their business to the City of Durham in 1872. The building, an old paper-mill, which they bought and enlarged at that time, was the building in which the business is still housed today. As the century turned, Thomas Harrison was succeeded by his sons, Arthur and Harry. Under their direction the company's work included the cathedral organs of Wells, Ely, Newcastle, Ripon, Manchester, Gloucester, Worcester, Exeter, Winchester and Durham itself. To this list must be added the Royal Albert Hall, Westminster Abbey, York Minster and Magdalen College, Oxford along with Trinity, St John's and King's College, Cambridge. Harrison and Harrison organs have also been sent to most parts of the world.

Harry's son, Cuthbert Temple Lane Harrison (1905-91), left his own indelible mark on the craft of English organ-building. Educated at Durham School and Exeter College, Oxford, he joined the family business in 1927 but was sacked two years later, his Uncle Arthur explaining that there was not enough room in the company for both of them. Cuthbert Harrison joined the Royal Tank Corps and served in India from 1929-37. Then his uncle died and he returned to help his father. On the outbreak of the Second World War, he became Major Harrison, Royal Artillery. Organ-building had, in any case, almost ceased during the hostilities. In 1945, however, he returned to Durham and it was not long before he became involved in what was quite a controversial project, the building of an organ for the new Royal Festival Hall. Three companies, including Harrison and Harrison, were invited to tender for the contract to build this instrument in time for the 1951 Festival of Britain. Realising the importance of this, Harrison's withdrew from the competition, refusing to be compromised on the issue of speed over quality. The other companies were also unable to meet the deadline and so the terms of the tender were altered. Harrison's was awarded the contract, and Cuthbert Harrison worked with Ralph Downes to produce a most remarkable instrument. Coventry Cathedral organ was another formidable Harrison achievement, in 1962.

Cuthbert Harrison became a great advocate of export, not only of organs but of craftsmen to restore and service them. He broke into the difficult North American market with considerable success and also won contracts in the Far East. He was, though, quintessentially a Durham man, lover of the county, city and, especially, the cathedral. For 40 years he was Secretary to the Friends of Durham Cathedral, and he was also a founder member of the organs advisory committee of the Council for the Care of Churches. Harrison was awarded the M.B.E. in 1980. The great tradition of which he was such an integral part be is still perpetuated by the company craftsmen today.

Across the road from the Harrison and Harrison factory, Allergate leads down the hill to the church of St Margaret of Antioch at the junction of Crossgate and South Street. Both streets are ancient thoroughfares. The earliest work in the church, which was originally a chapel of ease for St Oswald's, dates from the time of Bishop Hugh Pudsey, although the building was soon extended, the tower dating from the 15th century. Restoration was undertaken between 1865-80 by Hodgson Fowler.

South Street is one of Durham's most sought-after addresses, particularly the higher end of it which has the most magnificent views of the west end of the cathedral and castle. None of the buildings are particularly remarkable but they all

85.   The prior's corn mill, below Prebends' Bridge.

combine to create a most attractive entity. At the head of South Street is a little lane called Pimlico in which is The Grove, home of the actor Stephen Kemble during the early 19th century. A continuation of South Street leads to an often muddy footpath down to Prebends' Bridge. This three-arch bridge was designed by George Nicholson in 1777 to replace an earlier one of 1696 which was destroyed by the great flood of 1771. The bridge of 1696 itself had replaced a footbridge of 1574, before which date a ferry conveyed travellers across the Wear.

Environs and Epilogue

Not far from the centre of Durham City there are several sites of historic interest, without mention of which this book would be incomplete.

A few miles to the north-east of the city is the former colliery village of Bearpark, but in the days of the monks this was Beau Repaire, literally the beautiful retreat, one of the country homes of Durham's prior. Practically nothing remains to be seen today; all but a few stones have gone. The estate, established between 1200 and 1267, in which year the park was first enclosed, once covered an area of some 1,300 acres. The original fencing was replaced by a stone wall in 1311. It was Prior Bertram of Middleton who built the house and chapel at Beau Repaire when he retired in 1258, but there was a great deal of alteration in succeeding centuries; for example, a flushing latrine was incorporated at the end of the 13th century! The house was all but destroyed by invading Scots in 1640 and 1644; what was left standing was still to the height of the roof in 1787. Several generations of keepers in the park during the Middle Ages bore the surname 'Cowherd'.

Not far from Bearpark is the magnificent Ushaw College, more properly St Cuthbert's College, a most unlikely collection of buildings to be encountered in this part of the world, standing as they do on a high hilltop between the Rivers Browney and Deerness. The inside of the buildings is even more amazing than the exterior. The most outstanding is the Gothic-style chapel by Pugin, whose descendants also worked at Ushaw. This seminary's history dates back to the 16th century when there was founded at Douai in France a college to train Roman Catholic missionaries, who would work in England. In 1793, during the French Revolution, the college was seized by the authorities. The students sought and found refuge in England. In 1794 they assembled at Tudhoe, near Spennymoor in County Durham, at the school where the eminent Yorkshire naturalist Charles Waterton was educated. Later that year they went to Crook Hall near Lanchester, a few miles to the west of Durham, and in 1808 to their new home at Ushaw, building having begun there in 1804 following the site's purchase in 1799. The college tripled in size between the 1830s and the 1930s. The list of former students of Ushaw College is impressive by any standards. It is fascinating to note that one of those educated here was Francis Barraud, the man who went on to create the famous dog and gramophone trademark for His Master's Voice.

To the east of Durham is what remains of Sherburn Hospital, founded by Bishop Hugh Pudsey in 1181, to accommodate 65 monks and nuns who were suffering from leprosy. A master and three priests attended to their needs. When leprosy ceased to be the curse it had formerly been, patients suffering from other ailments were treated by the hospital, but it declined rapidly during the early years of the 16th century. The late Georgian and Victorian periods saw much rebuilding and renewed use of the hospital.

On the banks of the River Wear, near to Frankland Prison, stand the quiet ruins of Finchale Priory. It was here in about 1110 that a hermit called Godric settled. Born in Walpole, Norfolk, in 1065, he is said to have been a pedlar and a shipowner, travelling to, for example, Spain, Rome and the Holy Land. Godric is also alleged to have engaged in piracy at some stage in his nautical career and to have had the blood of several men on his hands. It was supposedly on a journey to Lindisfarne that he heard about St Cuthbert and determined to follow in his footsteps, as far as that was possible. To start himself on this road he travelled to Jerusalem. Forsaking the sea and back in England, he worked for some time in Norfolk and then moved first to Carlisle and next to the small village of Wolsingham in Weardale, Co. Durham. It was here that St Cuthbert told him, in a vision, that he was to go to Finchale, but where that was Godric did not know. He spent some time at Whitby, and then at the priory in Durham where he learned about Finchale, a bleak and deserted spot, infested with snakes and often flooded. He lived at first about a mile up-river from the present ruins. Godric's asceticism is well-known; he is said to have habitually sat naked in the Wear up to his neck all night long as a penance, to have worn nothing but sackcloth and to have eaten bread made of flour mixed with ashes, but only even then when it was several months old. A little stone church was built during his lifetime to cater for the visitors who came to see him; its foundations are within the chancel of the priory church, and it was here that he was buried when he died at Finchale in 1170, reputedly aged 105 years. It was Bishop Pudsey's son, Henry, who created a settlement here and in 1196 it became a priory for eight monks. In the 14th century, Finchale really became a holiday home for the monks of Durham Cathedral, four of them coming every three weeks to join the Prior of Finchale and his staff of four monks. Finchale Priory was one of the foundations hardest hit during Henry VIII's Dissolution of the Monasteries.

The university observatory, sited between Prebends' Bridge and the A167, was built in 1839, primarily as a home for astronomical instruments bought from a member of the Royal Astronomical Society. Durham was one of the observatories used to calculate the precise position of the planet Neptune. There are, of course, other buildings near Durham City which are well worth a visit. At the old mining village of Pittington, for example, there stands the beautiful and almost forgotten 12th-century church of St Laurence, some of it rebuilt by the ubiquitous Ignatius Bonomi. Still to be seen here are remnants of rare 12th-century wall-paintings showing scenes from the life of St Cuthbert.

Also near to Durham City are Brancepeth Castle and village, connected with (Bonnie) Bobbie Shaftoe, of folk-song fame, who lived just across the River Wear at Whitworth. Whether or not he really did go to sea with silver buckles at his knee will probably never be clearly established, but it is a piece of folklore of which the county is fiercely proud. The Bobbie, or Robert, Shaftoe celebrated in the song was actually one of Durham's first two Members of Parliament, returned in the 1761 election. It is said that Mary Bellasis, heiress to the Brancepeth fortunes, died of a broken heart when she was rejected by him in favour of her rival, Anne Duncombe. There is, of course, much more than this to be seen near Durham City. Here too are oriental

86. A mid-Victorian view of the city.

treasures and a branch of a Japanese university as well as a botanic garden. Less grand are Durham's hidden corners, which anyone who looks hard enough can find.

* * * * *

If, as Dr. Johnson said, 'When a man is tired of London he is tired of life', then perhaps that man should forsake the jaded metropolis to seek pastures new; to travel, in fact, to Durham to further his knowledge of England and to rekindle his love of life in one of the most beautiful cities in the world.

Appendix

The Bishops of Durham

Aldhun	995-1018
Eadmund	1020-1041
Eadred	1041
Ethelric	1042-1056
Ethelwin	1056-1071
Walcher	1072-1080
William de St Calais (St Carileph)	1081-1096
Ralph (Ranulf) Flambard	1099-1128
Geoffrey Rufus	1133-1140
William of St Barbara	1143-1152
Hugh Pudsey	1153-1195
Philip of Poitou	1197-1208
Richard Marsh	1217-1226
Richard le Poore	1228-1237
Nicholas of Farnham	1241-1249
Walter of Kirkham	1249-1260
Robert of Stichill	1261-1274
Robert de Insula	1274-1283
Anthony Bek	1283-1311
Richard of Kellawe	1311-1316
Lewis de Beaumont	1318-1333
Richard (Aungerville) of Bury	1333-1345
Thomas Hatfield	1345-1381
John Fordham	1381-1388
Walter Skirlaw	1388-1405
Thomas Langley	1406-1437
Robert Neville	1438-1457
Laurence Booth	1457-1476
William Dudley	1476-1483
John Sherwood	1484-1494
Richard Fox (Foxe)	1494-1501
William Senhouse	1502-1505
Christopher Bainbridge	1507-1508
Thomas Ruthall	1509-1522
Thomas Wolsey	1522-1528
Cuthbert Tunstall	1530-1552
(deposed, then restored)	

Cuthbert Tunstall 1559
James Pilkington 1561-1576
Richard Barnes 1577-1587
Matthew Hutton 1589-1595
Tobias Matthew 1595-1606
William James 1606-1617
Richard Neile 1617-1628
George Monteigne 1628
John Howson 1628-1632
Thomas Morton 1632-1659
John Cosin 1660-1672
Nathaniel, Lord Crewe 1674-1721
William Talbot 1721-1730
Edward Chandler· 1730-1750
Joseph Butler 1750-1752
Richard Trevor 1752-1771
John Egerton 1771-1787
Thomas Thurlow 1787-1791
Shute Barrington 1791-1826
William Van Mildert 1826-1836
Edward Maltby 1836-1856
Charles Thomas Longley 1857-1860
Henry Montague Villiers 1860-1861
Charles Baring 1861-1879
Joseph Barber Lightfoot 1879-1889
Brooke Foss Westcott 1890-1901
Handley Carr Glyn Moule 1901-1920
Herbert Hensley Henson 1920-1939
Alwyn Terrell Petre Williams 1939-1952
Arthur Michael Ramsey 1952-1956
Maurice Henry Harland 1956-1966
Ian Thomas Ramsey 1966-1972
John Stapylton Habgood 1973-1983
David Edward Jenkins 1984-

Bibliography

Bythell, D., *Durham Castle, University College, Durham* (Jarrold & Sons Ltd., Norwich, 1985)

City of Durham Trust, *Walks 1-4* (Macdonald Press Ltd., 1991)

Colgrave, B., *St Margaret's Church, Durham* (British Publishing Co., Gloucester, 1950)

Colgrave, B. & Gibby, C. W., *A Short Tour of Durham* (University Bookshop, S.P.C.K., Durham, 1984)

Cook, G. H. *The Story of Durham Cathedral* (Phoenix House Ltd., 1951)

Crosby, J. H., *Durham in Old Photographs* (Alan Sutton, Stroud, 1990)

Crosby, J. H., *Ignatius Bonomi of Durham, Architect* (City of Durham Trust, 1987)

Eden, Sir Timothy, *Durham,* The County Books series (Robert Hale, 1952)

Gibby, C. W., *A Short History of Durham* (Cherrett Brothers, 1975)

Hutchinson, W., *The History and Antiquities of the County Palatine of Durham* (3 vols., 1823)

Johnson, M., *Durham, Historic and University City* (Turnstone Ventures, 1987)

Mackenzie, E. & Ross, M., *An Historical, Topographical and Descriptive View of the County Palatine of Durham* (Mackenzie and Dent, Newcastle, 1834)

Mee, A., *The King's England: Durham* (Hodder & Stoughton, 1969)

Mills, J. A., *The Story of Bear Park (*Home Words, 1956)

Morris, R. J. B., *The City of Durham, its Town Hall, Guildhall and Civic Traditions* (Town Clerk, Durham, 1990)

Norris, R., *The Stained Glass in Durham Cathedral* (The Dean and Chapter of Durham, 1985)

Peers, C., *Finchale Priory, Durham* (H.M.S.O., 1937)

Pevsner, N. & Williamson, E., *The Buildings of England: County Durham* (Penguin Books, 1983)

Pocock, D. & Norris, R., *A History of County Durham* (Phillimore & Co., 1990)

Proud, K., *Great Northern Saints* (Discovery, 1983)

Proud, K., *The Prince Bishops of Durham* (Keybar, 1990)

Shea, W., *Carpet Making in Durham City* (Durham County Council, 1984)

Smith, D., *The Story of Sanctuary at Durham* (Frank Graham, Newcastle, 1971)

Stranks, C. J., *Durham Cathedral* (Pitkin Pictorials, Andover, 1970)

Stranks, C. J., *The Life and Death of St. Cuthbert* (S.P.C.K., 1987)

Stranks, C. J., *This Sumptuous Church* (S.P.C.K., 1983)

Sykes, J., *Local Records or Historical Records of Northumberland and Durham, Newcastle-upon-Tyne and Berwick-upon-Tweed* (1866)

Weston, W. J., *Durham* Cambridge County Geographies Series (1914)

White, Peter A., *Portrait of County Durham* (Robert Hale, London, 1967)

Index